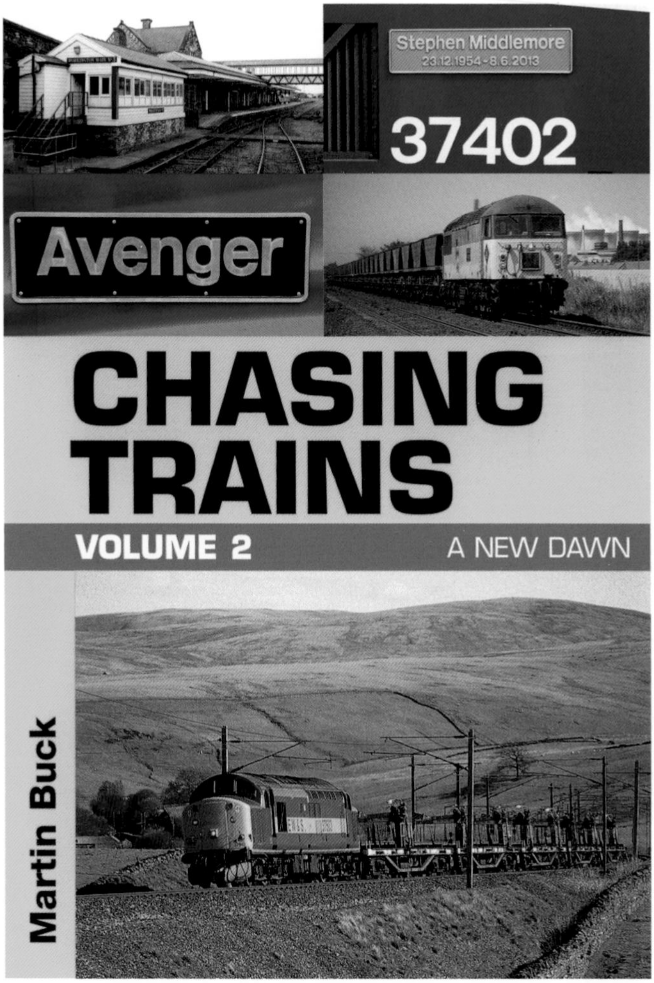

FREIGHTMASTER

PUBLISHING

CONTENTS

Published by :

Freightmaster Publishing
158 Overbrook
SWINDON
SN3 6AY

www.freightmasterpublishing.co.uk

First published : November 2020

ISBN : 978-0-9933129-4-6

Printed By :

Stephens & George
Goat Mill Road
Dowlais
MERTHYR TYDFIL
CF48 3TD

Cover Design : Martin Buck

All Images : Martin Buck, unless otherwise accredited.

A Hiatus

My active involvement in "*chasing trains*" around the rail network ended in May 1990, the last train I travelled on at that time was from Oxford to London Paddington with Class 50 No.50024 'Vanguard'.

It was the end of an era. No more trainspotting, that finished in June 1976, nor chasing diesel locos, which came to an end in 1984 (Class 46s) and in 1988 (Class 40s and Class 45s). I effectively became an 'armchair' enthusiast; I suppose it never goes away, railways are in my blood!

I started concentrating on other aspects of my life, like setting up a consultancy business offering a range of services, such as management, accountancy and taxation. In fact, this part of my business is still going strong and some of these clients have become good friends too.

As a pastime, I enjoy playing bridge and it was as a result of playing bridge that, unbeknown to me at the time, this would start another chapter in my life involving railways ....

From Little Acorns ....

In the summer of 1995, whilst playing bridge at my local club in Swindon, another player (who also shared an interest in railways) - who I will refer to as GJ - asked if I would be interested in a day out photographing trains. I politely declined, but he remained insistent and, after a few requests, I eventually relented and we had our day out.

For the record, on 19th July, we drove to a place called Milford Junction, near Selby in Yorkshire, where GJ had been to previously and said it was busy with freight - lots of coal trains! He was not wrong and I confess, it was a tremendous day out, seeing a procession of Class 56-hauled MGR coal trains shuttling back and forth between the Selby Coalfield and the Aire Valley power stations; Drax, Eggborough and Ferrybridge. I have replicated a few details from the day ....

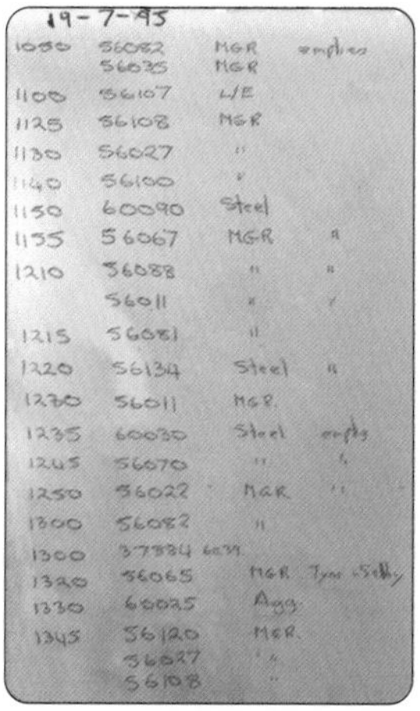

19-7-95

1050	56082	MGR	empties
	56035	MGR	
1100	56107	L/E	
1125	56108	MGR	
1130	56027	"	
1140	56100	"	
1150	60090	Steel	
1155	56067	MGR	"
1210	56088	"	"
	56011	"	"
1215	56081	"	
1220	56134	Steel	"
1230	56011	MGR	
1235	60030	Steel	empty
1245	56070	"	"
1250	56022	MGR	"
1300	56082	"	
1300	37884 LE		
1320	56065	MGR	Tyne - Selby
1330	60025	Agg	
1345	56120	MGR	
	56027	"	
	56108	"	

My Milford record

No.56011 approaches Milford Junction with MGR coal empties.

However, as the day panned out, it was not the trains that fascinated me, as good as this was, but a small booklet to which other enthusiasts were constantly refering, entitled *'Freightmaster'*.

This little booklet would ultimately change my working life for the next 25 years, quite simply .....

"Being in the right place, at the right time"

Martin Buck

2020

'The Next Step'

Whilst at Milford Junction, I jotted down details about *'Freightmaster'*, its cost, who compiled it, when it was published and where I could obtain a copy.

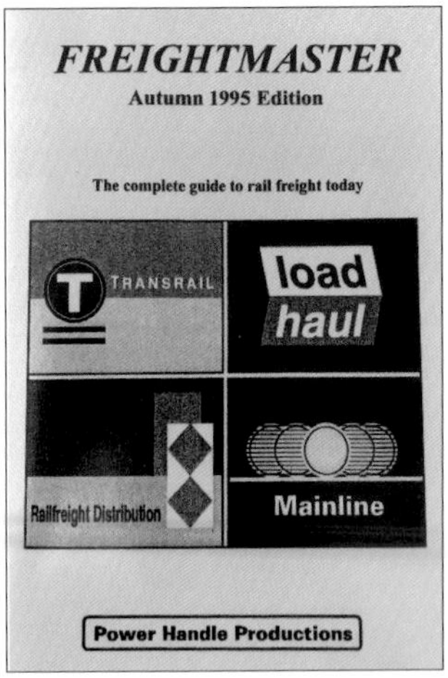

The booklet, at that time, consisted of 64 pages of typed timetables and hand-drawn regional maps, photocopied to order; its pages stapled in a laminated card cover. *'Freightmaster'* was complied by someone named Mark Rawlinson, who lived near Carnforth in Lancashire, next to the West Coast Main Line (WCML) and in close proximity to Morecambe Bay.

I thought it would be useful to keep track of freight movements around the country and wrote off with a cheque to purchase a year's subscription of four seasonal booklets. Lo and behold, after a couple of weeks without a word, I sent a reminder to see what was happening and, to my surprise, I received a telephone call from Mark, apologising for the delay, but having seen my business letterhead, he asked me a question ....

"*Would you be interested in managing my business*"?

I was staggered, to say the least, as most self-employed people are rather parochial, hands-on, who don't generally let outsiders into their business. It was a no-brainer and I gladly accepted .....

"the rest, as they say, is history".

The 'Freightmaster' years

Our arrangement suited Mark, leaving him to concentrate on developing *'Freightmaster'*, while I would manage in terms of marketing and production. From its humble origin, selling about a 1,000 photocopied booklets per annum, sales rocketed to **over 3,000 printed copies per quarter** at its peak.

'Freightmaster' grew in size to 160 pages with over 80 timetables. In 2010, we included full colour freight flow maps, plus an 'On Location' portfolio of superb colour images from the UK's best photographers depicting an area / route of interest.

First Freightmaster front cover in colour

One of My Tasks

Between 1996 - 2010, I went out myself to take photographs for possible use on the front cover of *'Freightmaster'*, seeking suitable locations which would lend themselves to 'portrait' orientation, rather than the more usual 'landscape' format.

This took me to all parts of the rail network, visiting a location on one or more occasions to get the required shot.

As you can probably imagine, this task became more and more difficult as time went on, bearing in mind that a front cover image could not be some mundane, run of the mill, image. I was looking for something with impact, newsworthy, a specific class of loco or an interesting commodity.

When the 'On Location' feature started in 2010, I was able to stop doing this and use one or more of images contributed by invited guest photographers.

In 1997, ***'Class One'*** was launched, the passenger equivalent to 'Freightmaster', with selective timetables listing loco-hauled passenger services, plus loco diagrams. This title ceased to be viable after the 2003 timetable change when diesel and electric locos were replaced on Virgin Cross Country and Virgin West Coast services. Finally, in 2020 and some 25 years later, *'Freightmaster'* published its **100th** edition.

What Came Next

Mark developed an online version of *'Freightmaster'* which also included an inter-active Forum, where members can share information, access TOPS lists and a lot more interesting details pertaining to freight - in short, this has gone on to become, most probably, the best of its type on the market.

We also set out to expand the business by compiling and publishing our own series of railway books, which include:

'Line By Line' : a comprehensive set of 5 guides on famous railway routes, detailing:

- a 5-mile section per page, complete with an illustration.
- mileages
- track layout
- gradient profile

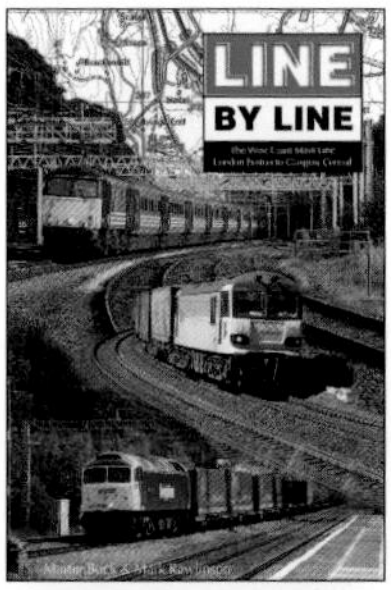

1st) **West Coast Main Line**
London Euston to Glasgow Central
Plus, the Northampton Loop

2nd) **Great Western Main Line**
London Paddington - Penzance
via Bristol Temple Meads and Westbury

3rd) **East Coast Main Line**
London King's Cross - Edinburgh Waverley
Plus, Edinburgh Waverley - Carstairs

4th) **The Midland Route**
London St. Pancras - Glasgow Central
via Leeds, Settle & Carlisle, Dumfries

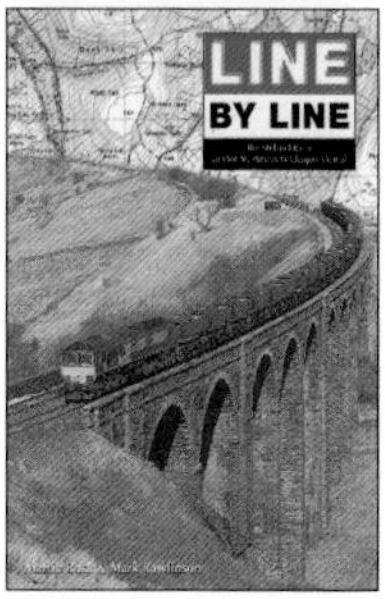

5th) **The Scottish Highlands**
Glasgow Queen Street - Oban
Crianlarich - Fort William
Fort William - Mallaig
Glasgow Queen Street - inverness
Plus, Perth - Aberdeen

Wagon Recognition : (1)
A full colour, illustrated, encyclopedia of all current wagons working on the rail network.

Wagon Recognition : (2)
A fully illustrated guide of departmental wagons and On Track Plant

Individual Titles

It's certainly been busy times, as well as the *'Line By Line'* series and two '*Wagon Recognition*' books, I have compiled some titles of my own, 'thumbnail' cover images are shown below:

Freightmaster Review 1994 - 2005	:	Illustrated review of freight flows, motive power and freight operating companies.
Railfreight Yearbook	:	Review of freight in 2005.
Loco-Hauled Yearbook	:	Review of freight in 2006.
Line By Line	:	The Settle & Carlisle Railway Line. 25th Anniversary special : 1989 - 2014. Foreword written by The Right Honourable Michael Portillo.
Wagon Recognition	:	A combined, illustrated guide: Wagons, departmental wagons and On Track Plant. Sponsored by VTG, Europe's leading wagon leasers.
Loco Review	:	**10 editions** between 2008 - 2017 A Review of freight, locos, freight flows, etc.

Compilation

When I set out to produce a new book, I always start with a template, similar in format to the book at which you are now looking and reading. Its production is a complete 'Volvo system', from start to finish, whereby I design the layout, write the text and format the images (which all have to be CMYK TIFF). This results in producing a **P.D.F.** file (**P**ortable **D**ocument **F**ormat), which encapsulates all the text, fonts and images. This file is uploaded to my printers (Stephens & George in Merthyr Tydfil), who create a print file, then print the book. It is then my task to advertise the book and sell it.

'Photographs'

As a publisher compiling railway titles, this has enabled me to go out and take photographs for the various titles, ranging from cover shots for *Freightmaster*, location shots for *'Line By Line'* or simply wagon types for *'Wagon Recognition'*; an eclectic mix of photographs and all my adventures have been enjoyable.

I have included some of my favourite images and here's a few anecdotes of my endeavours ....

"Every Picture Tells a Story"

November 1998

'Under the Wires'

Some photographers avoid taking photographs 'under the wires', preferring open and uncluttered views. I see this as a challenge and therefore sought out locations to demonstrate this.

This image became the front cover of the 'Winter 1998 / 1999' edition of Freightmaster (FM) and is taken, whilst sitting on the perimeter wall, at Rugby station.

ReS liveried Class 86/2 No.86241 'Glenfiddich" hurries along the Down Fast line with 5F91, the 14:39 Euston Downside Carriage Sidings - Warrington RMT empty mail vans.

Historically, Rugby station opened 1885 and, following the former Rugby Central station on the now-abandoned Great Central Railway route, became Rugby's only station.

The station underwent an extensive upgrade during 2006 – 2008, with extra platforms added, however the majority of columns and canopies seen here were demolished.

April 2002

'A 'Shed' - also Under the Wires'

In the EWS era, the Class 66/0 'shed' became the mainstay of their freight operations; despised by many, as they replaced favourites, like 31s, 33s, 37s, etc.

Due to their commonality throughout the land, I tried to avoid using an image of a 'shed' on a front cover but, as time went on, thought it was time to do so. After all, somebody likes these General Motors locos, don't they?

In the beautiful Lune Gorge, No 66163 passes Beck Foot, close to the M6 Motorway, slowing to enter the Up Goods Loop at Grayrigg to allow a passenger express to pass.

The 'shed' is running today as 6Z27, Ayr - Ironbridge power station (ps) loaded MGR coal, which is running in the path of the scheduled 6M40, Ayr - Rugeley ps.

It may be a 'shed', but I think the composition works really well.

FM No.25.

June 1999

'Not a *Waste* of Time ...."

By this time, the 'Avon Binliner' was booked for an EWS Class 66, before which the train could turn up at Swindon with a variety of motive power - 37s, 47s, 50s, 58s, for example.

It was also a reliable runner, usually arriving around 12:15hrs -12:30hrs, where it would sit until its booked departure time of 13:30hrs.

On this particular occasion, I was driving to the station car park in Swindon and saw Class 58 No.58014 sitting in the Down Goods line awaiting a new crew.

I changed my plans and drove to Bristol and photographed it there - I already knew my vantage point, which would be where the elevated A4320 flyover spans the Great Western Main Line.

It was worth it, standing on a narrow walkway, No.58017 passes North Somerset junction with 4B05, Bath - Westerleigh empty 'Binliner, a portion off 4V13 ex-Calvert landfill site.

FM Summer 1999

September 2007

'New Kid On The Block'

One interesting development saw Amec Spie move into the railfreight market transporting timber for Kronospan in Chirk, using Virgin Class 57/3s; locos normally used to haul diverted West Coast passenger services or as a 'Thunderbird' rescue loco.

As the loaded timber train did not reach Warrington (where I was photographing) until around 17:00hrs, I had to decide on a better location for a 'portrait' photograph.

I opted for Helsby on the Warrington - Chester line because the sun would be in the right position, plus there was the added bonus of semaphore signals, which were always worth seeking out.

No.57303 'Alan Tracey' approaches Helsby with 6J37, Carlisle Yard - Chirk loaded timber.

FM No.47.

June 1997 **"Class 31 Swansong"** FM Summer 1997 *(opposite)*

I knew that by the end of 1997, the remaining Class 31 in traffic would be withdrawn, making this the last summer to catch them in action. This prompted an idea for a cover shot and I thought that overlooking Colwyn Bay would be a good bet. So, I set off early doors from Swindon for the long drive to North Wales, plumping for a scenic route via Central Wales, skirting Snowdonia, to Colwyn Bay. I had plenty of time, as my chosen train wasn't expected to pass until around 11:30hrs. The location would overlook where the railway line crossed over the A55 trunk road.

I arrived off the A547 Abergele Road and parked the car in Tan Y Lan Road and walked to my vantage point.

It could not have turned out better; a glorious sunny day, splendid views of Colwyn Bay and a pair of Class 31s turning up on 6F11, Penmaenmawr - Warrington Arpley ballast, loaded in YGA 'Seacow' and YGH 'Sealion' bogie ballast hoppers. The leading loco is Mainline blue No.31407 and the second loco is No.31308 sporting 'Dutch' civil engineer's livery of grey with a yellow band.

The only downside; afterwards, I developed a bad migraine which delayed my journey home for a couple of hours. It did get marginally better and I decided to make a start and go back via a more direct and faster route using the A55, M6, M5, but I still felt nauseous, I remember stopping several times on the way.

March 2003

'If You Don't Succeed ...."

Due to the high value of the vehicles, Jaguar cars are conveyed in vandal-proof enclosed car carriers. Wagons from Halewood and Castle Bromwich are combined at Washwood Heath, going forward as one train - 4O20 to Southampton Eastern Docks.

I specifically wanted to photograph this train and chose Eastleigh as a good location. In the end, it all came good, and No.66170 is seen snaking out of Eastleigh station and onto the main line with train 4020 in its wake.

In fact, this image was achieved at the ***sixth*** time of asking, previous attempts had all been thwarted by a mixture of a no show or cloud masking the sun at the vital moment.

Fortunately, Eastleigh is not too far from Swindon!

FM No.29

July 2007

'The New Order'

In the past 12 months leading up to this image, the freight scene had been enhanced by many new wagons;

'HOAs' : EWS bogie aggregate hoppers.
'HIAs' : FHH bogie limestone hoppers
'HYAs' : GBRf bogie coal hoppers
'IWAs' : Timber carrier conversions.
'KFAs'

Class 66/6 No.66624 hauls a rake of new FHH-branded HIA wagons through Wellingborough, running as 6M17, Croft - Neasden.

There was also a white liveried version of the HIA, to distinguish between different flows.

FM No.46.

January 2006 'GBRf" ....

(opposite)

From the new year, GBRf agreed to advertise with us and I wanted to include one of their trains on a front cover - the trouble was, which train and where? I could not think of too many places that would lend a shot but, fortunately, I struck lucky, coming across a GBRf departmental working that I wasn't even aware of.

I was in residence by the side of the A453 which links Nottingham and the M1 motorway, principally to photograph some trains on the Midland Main Line with a backdrop of the cooling towers at Ratcliffe-on-Soar ps. East Midlands Parkway has since been built as a 'Park & Ride' station adjacent to Milepost 118.

A pair of GBRf Class 66/7 'Bluebirds' came into view hauling a rake of empty JNA 'Falcon' open ballast wagons. The working was a special 6Z91, Stapleford & Sandiacre - Peterborough Yard, hauled by No.66701 'Whitemoor' and No.66702 'Blue Lightning'.

FM No.40

50
66701
118

September 2000

'Sonning'

Sonning Cutting is on the site of the original Broad Gauge, GWML, built by Isambard Kingdom Brunel between 1838 - 1840. It's about a mile in length, lying between Reading and Twyford.

I found this to be an ideal location for viewing trains because of its impressively steep sides and with views from a number of bridges.

On this particular visit, I positioned myself on the A4, London Road bridge, looking east towards Warren Road bridge.

Warren Road bridge has a central arched span of about 65ft, made of wrought iron, with red and purple GWR brick used for the abutments etc..

In this view, Mendip Rail Class 59/0 No.59002 'Alan J Day' proceeds slowly through the cutting on the Down Slow line with 6V18, Hither Green - Whatley Quarry empty Hanson bogie aggregate hoppers.

The loco sports a green and orange livery branded for 'Mendip Rail', which was a joint venture by Foster Yeoman and Hanson (formerly ARC) to run the heavy aggregate trains from the Mendips.

FM No.37.

May 2009

'Cherry Red'

I should start by saying that 'Cherry Red' does not refer in this instance to a track of the same name by the rock band 'Groundhogs'.

English, Welsh & Scottish Railway (EWS) officially handed over the reins to DB Schenker (DBS) from 1st January 2009. The old Wisconsin Central style maroon & gold livery became a thing of the past as DBS adopt a striking cherry red and grey livery, based on the famous colours of the German parent company, Deutsche Bahn.

No.66152 became the first 'shed' to receive the new livery and, on 5th May 2009, it made its first visit to Swindon; an event I wanted to record for posterity.

The loco is seen on the old Highworth branch, about to couple up to the first of four MBAs loaded with scrap. From here, the wagons will be propelled to Cocklebury yard but, due to limited capacity in the terminal, No.66152 will have to make between 3 - 5 trips in order to complete the full trainload.

No.66152 will finally leave Swindon in the evening with 6M73, the 20:50 Swindon Cocklebury - Liverpool Alexandra Dock.

FM No.55.

August 2007

'Second Time of Asking' ....

On my way home from Teesside after spending a few days photographing wagons for the new '*Wagon Recognition*', I decided to stop off at Milford Junction. My aim was to get a shot of a new GBRf coal flow from Tyne Dock to Drax ps, booked for a GBRf Class 66/7 loco.

The train was due to pass at 11:15hrs and I was set up, ready and waiting .... bang on time, the train arrived but, as I depressed the shutter, my camera jammed and I missed the shot. I was not amused, knowing that I would have to return.

The weather forecast for 9th August 2007 was fabulous and, without a cloud in the sky, I decided to drive north for a shot of this coal train, plumping for Knottingley to secure the shot - please bear in mind that I had never obtained a shot from here before, but I was convinced I would succeed!

As it turned out, I got my shot - GBRf 'Metronet' Class 66/7 No.66719 'Metro-Land' (above) passes through Knottingley station with 6H93, the 06:51 Tyne Dock - Drax loaded coal. FM No.48

"Chasing 37s"

January 1997

'Vinegar Joe'

This turned out to be the first front cover to feature a Class 37 and I opted for the location of East Usk, Newport, with the backdrop of Llanwern steelworks, which at the time still had working blast furnaces.

The only trouble with this one, was that the train did not pass me until 15:30hrs when the sun was already low in the sky. I just about managed a shot of No.37706 hauling a rake of empty TTA, 2-axle, acetic acid tanks, which formed 6V14, Hull Saltend - Baglan Bay.

I had a beautiful, late afternoon, drive home with glorious sunshine spilling over the Severn estuary as I crossed the original suspension bridge carrying the M4 motorway. I was completely unaware of my speed which, unfortunately, the police were not, and I was booked for speeding!

FM Spring 1997.

May 1997

'A Class Act'

In the summer of 1997, we decided to publish a passenger equivalent of 'Freightmaster', which we called 'Class One', listing details of all loco-hauled passenger services in the UK.

We chose busy stations and a handful of scenic locations to satisfy the photographers among our readers.

For each train service listed, there was the departure / passing time, headcode and details of the booked traction. We later included loco-diagrams for most loco-hauled workings: 37s, 47s and 86/s as well, ; details which could not be gleaned from other sources.

I drove to North Wales for the first cover shot and Abergele & Pensarn was my chosen location. Class 37/4 No.37402 departs with 1K58, the 07:37 Holyhead - Crewe.

The signal box is a London & North Western Railway type 4 design fitted with a 60 lever tumbler frame, opening in July 1902. It is no longer operational, but is Grade II listed.

CLASS ONE : Summer 1997.

April 2002

'Burton 'Trip"

Sometimes, potential cover-shots don't always turn out as planned, although I was pleased with this result.

The aim was to photograph the 'Burton Trip', which was an 'Enterprise' working rostered for an EWS Class 47. The diagram was:

- 6D36, Bescot - Burton on Trent
- 6D77, Burton on Trent - Toton
- 6G77, Toton - Bescot.

However, although it was great to see a 37, I did not use the shot as it would otherwise have given a false impression of what the motive power was on this train.

With the yard lights standing tall, No.37669 in EWS maroon & gold livery, marshals SPA 2-axle open plate wagons loaded with steel coil. The train arrived as 6D36 from Bescot and will proceed to Toton via Stenson Junction and the 'freight-only' line to Sheet Stores Junction.

No.37669 was withdrawn from service in September 2007.

May 2009

'In the Cutting'

Technically, 6D78, Healey Mills - Neville Hill (Leeds) loaded fuel oil tanks was 'booked' for a Class 56 loco but, as a 37 was spare at Healey Mills on the day, the operators decided to use it on this short 'trip'.

Complete with miniature snow ploughs and a 'domino' headcode panel, No.37174 passes through the impressive cutting at Horbury, south-west of Wakefield, with 6D78, Healey Mills - Neville Hill, ex-Lindsey oil refinery on Humberside.

A photograph is only possible of eastbound trains, as the Up line was too close to the side of the cutting. The sun is in the right position for a morning shot and I had a choice of eastbound trains to choose from:

- 6M89, Dewsbury - Earles (cement)
- 6E32, Preston Docks - Lindsey (bitumen)
- 6E06, Bredbury - Roxby (GMC 'Binliner')

FM No.33.

September 2000

'Old Colwyn'

After capturing a pair of Class 31s on the Penmaenmawr - Warrington Arpley ballast, I decided to stay a little longer and photograph a Class 37 on of the 'Bangor' diagrams, albeit now with a Class 37 and not a Class 40, like in the early '80s.

And with such stunning views, why not?

Class 37/4 No.47429, in Regional Railways livery of blue and grey, off-set by a white and turquoise waist height band, approaches with 1K61, the 10:22 Bangor - Crewe.

The full diagram (CD 893) for the loco was:

- 1K53, 07:39 Chester - Crewe
- 1D60, 08:17 Crewe - Bangor
- 1K61, 10:22 Bangor - Crewe
- 1D69, 12:20 Crewe - Holyhead
- 1K71, 14:36 Holyhead - Crewe
- 1D79, 17:17 Crewe - Bangor
- 2D73, 20:22 Bangor - Chester

The workings were quite intense with five diagrams running daily between Monday and Saturday.

April 2002

'Bescot 'Trip"

This shot was intended to be a 'back up' shot in case the earlier photograph of No.37669 at Burton on Trent did not work out.

This is Kingsbury, Warwickshire, a location close to Junction 9 of the M42 where, from the vantage point of Trinity Road bridge, there are good views of southbound freight traffic on the Birmingham - Derby main line.

No.37669 is working 6G77, Toton - Bescot 'Enterprise' trip with a consist of fuel oil tanks and bogie steel carriers.

The lines leading off to the right behind the cabin lead to three busy terminals:

- Kingsbury oil terminal.
- EMR scrap metal recycling plant.
- Birch Coppice intermodal terminal.

June 2001

'Off The Peg'

This is Park Junction, Newport, where semaphore signals control the double track to Ebbw Junction and the single line to Gaer Junction on the right.

Class 37/4 No.47419 'waits for the road' to Ebbw Junction with 6B50, Machen Quarry - Newport Alexandra Dock Junction loaded ballast. For operational purposes, the train is running in top 'n' tail mode with No.47412 (out of view) at the rear.

The train would normally run via Gaer Junction to East Usk Yard, reverse, and the loco at the rear, in this instance, No.37412 would proceed to ADJ yard.

However, the single spur between Park Junction and Gaer Junction is out of use, necessitating in 6B50 running to Ebbw Junction and onto the 'Down Relief' of the South Wales main line, where No.37412 will lead the consist into the yard.

March 1999

'Rugby Coal'

This is an interesting piece of railway, where the Up main line is at a lower level than the Down line at Patchway, Bristol.

Class 37/7 No.37718 has emerged from the eastern portal of Patchway New Tunnel (1 mile long) with MEA, 2-axle open box wagons, loaded with imported coal.

The working is 6M14, Newport Docks - Rugby although the flow can also originate from Avonmouth and be Class 56-hauled.

Unfortunately, not long after this picture was recorded, the working went over to EWS Class 66 operation, like so many flows did, as more and more of the dreaded 'sheds' came on stream.

The loco became part of a Class 37/7 sub class, which was a refurbished loco, where the main generator was replaced by an alternator. It had regeared (CP7) bogies with ballast weights added.

No.37718 was one of the 37s sent to Spain in April 2001 to work on a high speed line, returning only to be cut up in 2015.

April 1997 **'Shap Attack'**

This is Greenholme, where the WCML climbs at a steady 1 in 75 from Tebay to Shap Summit, 916ft above sea level. There was a steady flow of southbound freight, but nothing northbound between 10:00 hrs and 17:00hrs. So, when No.37503 appeared working an engineer's train, this was a bonus. You will note that the branding in the gold band is E W & S, but the '&' was soon dropped, becoming simply EWS.

This image did not make the front cover of Freightmaster, but definitely did so for this title!

July 2001 **'Nearly Bowled'**

Barnetby in South Humberside was a rail enthusiast's mecca; lots of freight, semaphore signals, which attracted trainspotters and photographers from far and wide, like bees round a honey pot. I positioned myself on the footbridge at the station to capture No.37667 working a lengthy 6D65, Doncaster - Immingham 'Enterprise', which approached so slowly that Class 56 No.56064 working a 7C75, Immingham - Scunthorpe loaded coal nearly spoilt the shot. However, I think the result turned out better than I expected. *FM No.24.*

"Firsts"

October 1996

This image was my choice for the first Freightmaster front cover in full colour - taken at Highworth Junction, Swindon.

A two-tone grey, Railfreight Distribution branded Class 47, No.47229, pulls out of Cocklebury Sidings with 6M03, the 08:15 Swindon (Rover) - Longbridge, conveying body panels for the main Rover factory.

The consist is KSA 'Cube' bogie wagons, purpose-built by Arbel Fauvet, France, in 1995 for this service. However, following the demise of Rover, the wagons were initially transferred to Scotland to work W H Malcolm intermodal traffic from Grangemouth to Daventry.

This did not last long and the remaining wagons were either scrapped or converted to timber carriers.

FM Winter 1996 / 1997.

June 2009

'Cherry Red 59/2'

For the first time in April 2010, we introduced colour inside 'Freightmaster', well, most of it anyway, in an attempt to spruce up the Book and provide our loyal readers with some exclusive content not found in the online version:

'On Location' turned into a regular feature in each issue. The aim was to provide a photographic guide illustrating the freight services to be seen in and around a Freightmaster timetable, along with listing the best vantage points.

The first location was Westbury - centre of Mendip Rail operations and an ideal place to see all the different liveried Class 59/2s and associated rolling stock.

I wanted a striking front cover so I opted for the first Class 59/2 to receive D B Schenker 'cherry-red' livery, albeit not at Westbury, but at Crofton on a Mendip Rail stone service.

No.59206 'John F. Yeoman' sweeps round Crofton Curve with 6V18, Hither Green - Whatley Quarry empty bogie stone hoppers.

FM No.50.

"A Striking Livery"

The long-awaited entry of Fastline in the power station coal market took place in May 2008. The services were rather hybrid as only a handful of new fastline IIA wagons had been delivered and their own Class 66/3 locos had yet to arrive in the UK. Initially, rakes were formed of spare GBRf HYAs and hauled by a Class 66/7 loco working from Daw Mill colliery and Hatfield mine to Ratcliffe power station.

I was keen to photograph this new service and thought long and hard about which location to use and opted for Whitacre Junction, which was east of Birmingham on the Water Orton - Nuneaton main line. It was about a two-hour drive from Swindon arriving there by way of the M5 and M42 motorways for the best part of the journey.

Having run to Saltley to run-round, brand new Class 66/3 No.66301 passes Whitacre Junction with loaded hoppers, both GBRf and Fastline IIAs, running as 6D03, the 10:28 Daw Mill - Ratcliffe. The train will run via Nuneaton, Hinckley and Leicester. The new livery certainly improved the aesthetics of a Class 66 loco.

For some reason, I did not use this image for a front cover shot, probably as the location had been previously used to feature a GBRf intermodal service from the recently re-opened Hams Hall intermodal terminal.

'Grids'

Setting The Scene

On 9th June 1976, I saw the last loco I needed to complete seeing all the locos listed in my Ian Allan Locoshed Book and, at this time, the new Class 56s had not yet entered service ....

- the Romanian built examples were still in Romania.
- the British built locos had yet to be completed / enter traffic.

In fact, when I visited Doncaster Works on 6th June 1976, all 56s were in the very early stages of construction - just an empty shell mounted on a wooden support, no engine unit or bogies. Luckily for me, these did not count, as you could only do so for a complete loco - phew!

Historical Perspective

The British Rail Class 56 is a Type 5 diesel loco designed for heavy freight work, fitted with a Ruston-Paxman power unit developing 3,250 bhp (2,423 kW) and has a Co-Co wheel arrangement. The fleet was introduced between 1976 and 1984 with a total of 135 examples manufactured.

The first 30 locos (Nos.56001 - 56030) were built by Electroputere in Romania, but these were poorly constructed and many were withdrawn from service early for extensive rebuilding before re-entering revenue service. The construction of the remaining 105 locos was split between:

Doncaster Works : Nos.56031 - 56115. Crewe Works : Nos.56116 - 56135.

The first Doncaster constructed 'Grid' entered service in May 1977 and the first Crewe loco, March 1983. Enthusiasts nicknamed the Class 56s 'Gridirons', or just simply 'Grids', due to the grid-like horn cover on the loco's cab ends.

On 4th August 1976, Nos.56001 and 56002 were shipped from Zeebrugge to Harwich and on 7th August they were towed to Tinsley, after which trials commenced on the Settle & Carlisle Line.

First View

Looking back through my notes, I first 'spotted' a Class 56 in August 1976 when No.56001 and No.56002 were stabled on Tinsley MPD. My first photograph featured No.56050 at Crofton on the 'Berks & Hants' line in September 1985.

UK Ownership

After the privatisation of British Rail, the entire class passed to English Welsh & Scottish Railways (EWS) in 1995, following the purchase of Loadhaul, Mainline and Transrail freight companies. However, withdrawals commenced in the 1990s, with the last one withdrawn in March 2004.

DB Cargo : (2011) : (ex-DB Schenker / ex-EWS) placed the remaining 33, stored, 56s up for sale.

Fastline : (2006) : Nos 56045 and 56124 purchased and returned to service as No.56301 and No.56302, respectively. Fastline ceased operating in 2010.

FM Rail : (2009) : No.56125 returned to service as No.56303. The loco transferred to RVEL (FM Rail's successor) and repainted in Great Western Railway green livery to celebrate GWR 175 in 2010.

British American Railway Services / Devon & Cornwall Railways

(2009) : Initially under Hanson traction ownership, formerly preserved No.56057 returned to service as No.56311, whilst No.56003 became No.56312; the latter in a striking purple livery with green 'ARTEMIS' branding on the bodyside.

UK Rail Leasing : (2013) : Leicester-based UK Rail Leasing operates Class 56s on a spot-hire basis. They acquired a number of locos from DB Cargo that had previously been exported abroad for work on the construction of high speed rail lines. Nos.56081, 56098 and 56104 returned to operational use in July 2014 in unbranded original Railfreight Grey livery.

Colas Rail : (2014) : Initially, Colas purchased Nos.56078 / 087 / 094 / 105 and 113 from DB Cargo for work on infrastructure trains, timber traffic and petroleum products.

GBRf : (2018) : GB Railfreight acquired 16 locos owned by UK Rail Leasing, some may be returned to traffic, whilst others will be re-engineered. The locos were previously owned by DB Cargo and subsequently hired to Fertis, for high speed rail construction trains in France.

Barnetby (above) : *Coal sector No.56090 passes Barnetby East signal box and enters the station with a loaded MGR coal train, running as 7G08, Immingham - Scunthorpe steelworks. Now that the semaphore signals have gone, replaced by MAS colour lights, the magic of Barnetby went with them!* (09/95)

Middlesbrough (opposite) : *Viewed from the top of the A19 Flyover, Middlesbrough, EWS liveried Class 56 No.56087 'ABP Port of Hull' heads along the Up Goods No.1 line with a lengthy rake of empty steel carriers (mostly bogie bolsters and 2-axle open wagons), which form 6G50, Tees Dock - Tees Yard. In the background (top left) is the Newport Transporter Bridge.* (07/03)

Blyth Cambois

Blyth Cambois depot was situated on the west side of the branch line from Bedlington Junction to Blyth Docks.

It opened in 1968, replacing steam sheds at Percy Main, North Blyth and South Blyth.

During the 1970s & 1980s, Type 3 Class 37s were the staple motive power, replaced by Class 56s from 1981.

Nine Class 56s and one Class 08 shunting loco were required to service the 20 daily train diagrams.

By 1987, Blyth became a sub-shed of Toton and finally closed in 1994, when Loadhaul concentrated train crew and loco maintenance at Tyne Yard.

BR Blue, Large Logo, 'Grids'

(top left) : No.56132 'Fina Energy'.

(middle) : *No.56111.*

(below) :

No.56124 'Blue Circle Cement'
No.56133 Crewe Locomotive Works'.

Sunderland South Dock

The old steam shed at Sunderland South Dock was still in use in the 1980s, where locos were stabled in between duties working coal trains in the County Durham coalfield. However, as the work went and the mines closed, the locos were based elsewhere and the depot closed in 1994.

(above) : *No.56126 sits proudly in the yard as two other 'grids' poke their noses out of the old steam shed. (09/88)*

Colton Junction

This particular vantage point is a short walk across the fields on a public bridleway east of the village of Colton, five miles south of York. A footpath leads to a footbridge, a short distance north of Colton Junction, which offers excellent views looking north. The nearside tracks run to Church Fenton while the furthest lines are the ECML to Doncaster.

(above) : *EWS maroon & gold livery No.56051 heads along the Up Leeds main line with a loaded MGR, which is probably imported coal from Redcar to Ferrybridge power station. Of course, without the benefit of TOPS or 'Real Time Trains', it was almost impossible to identify coal trains, which ran to a weekly trainplan. (07/00)*

(left) : *It's a light payload today for Transrail Class 56 No.56070, as it speeds through Milford Junction with 6M26, the 11:35 Tees Yard - Warrington Arpley 'Enterprise', comprising a single bogie bolster steel carrier - hardly seems worth it!* (07/95)

(below) : *No.56068, with prominent red painted buffer beam and black coal sector diamond decals, crosses from Milford Down Sidings with HAA hoppers fitted with a canopy, which will be propelled into Milford West Sidings.*

There are a variety of these MGR-style of hoppers and a summary is given below. (09/95)

Wagons

The 'HAA' 2-axle MGR coal hopper became the most iconic 'modern' British wagon, designed to haul coal in non-stop 'merry-go-round' trips between mines and power stations; set up to be able to load and unload at slow speed without a need to stop the train. The design dates from the 1960s and 11,162 MGR hoppers were built, some used to carry limestone to line blast furnaces at steelworks.

These wagons dominated coal traffic before high-capacity 'HTA' and 'HHA' bogie hoppers came on stream from 2000 onwards. From the original 'HAA'-style hopper with automechanical discharge capability, variant designs followed, thus:

HAA	Original design in 1964. No canopy or modifications.	45 mph loaded / 55 mph empty.
HBA	Original design + Canopy.	60 mph loaded / 60 mph empty.
HCA	Original design + Canopy.	45 mph loaded / 60 mph empty.
HDA	Final batch of 450 MGR coal hoppers, built in 1982.	60 mph loaded / 60 mph empty.
HFA	Original design + Aerodynamic Canopy fitted.	45 mph loaded / 60 mph empty.
HMA	Original design + Modified Brakes.	45 mph loaded / 60 mph empty.
HNA	Original design + Modified Brakes + Canopy.	45 mph loaded, 60 mph empty.

After a hiatus away from railways, this was to be my taste of what I had been missing - a visit to Milford Junction - a veritable haven for loads of MGR coal trains hauled by Class 56s from the Gascoigne Wood Mine to Drax, Eggborough and Ferrybridge power stations, although the lion share of which went to Drax.

The location is near the village of Monk Fryston, a vantage point being a bridge which crosses the four running lines at this point, on a quiet lane leading from the main A63 Selby road to South Milford. Perfect, the odd car or farmer's tractor being the only distraction from the procession of coal trains passing below.

Milford Junction is strategically situated with lines converging from the direction of York, Gascoigne Wood, Castleford, Moorthorpe, Knottingley and Doncaster.

Historically, there used to be a railway station here - Milford Junction - on the York and North Midland Railway, south of the south-east connecting chord of 1840 between that railway and the Leeds and Selby Railway. The station closed in October 1904 and the station buildings demolished in 1960. At the time of my visit, the old 'Up' platform (see image below) was still in situ, a convenient place to change both train crew and locos.

Milford Junction

(above) : *Loadhaul 'grid' No.56027 is heading towards the Gascoigne Wood complex at Milford Junction with a rake of empty HAA MGR coal hoppers. The loco is passing under the bridge, which is the vantage point mentioned in the text, while the other bridge carries the main A63 road to Selby.*

I am actually standing on the old platform of Milford Junction railway station. (07/95)

(above) : *Having already returned from Drax earlier in the morning with empty HAAs, No.56027 now heads back the way it came with loaded HAAs, destined for either Drax or Eggborough.* *(07/95)*

(opposite) : *The driver of EWS liveried Class 56 No.56018 pulls hard on the power handle as the loco accelerates towards the camera with loaded MEAs destined for Clitheroe. The MEAs were a welcome distraction from a diet of HAAs, although this train (6M79) necessitated MEAs, as there are no automatic discharge facilities at the cement works, thus precluding HAAs. In this view, Milford West Sidings are crammed with both the old style HAA wagons and the new EWS, HTA bogie hoppers.* *(03/03)*

(below) : *Black diamond sub-sector decals are quite appropriate for locos assigned to haul trains of coal, a form of carbon just as valuable as a diamond. No.56087 chugs away nicely as it approaches Milford Junction with a rake of empty HAA hoppers from either Drax or Eggborough power station.* *(09/95)*

56018
25

GASCOIGNE WOOD

Within the Selby Coalfield, Gascoigne Wood was the largest mine, comprising five interconnecting deep mines within a 20 mile area. When the coal was brought to the surface using twin drift shafts at Gascoigne Wood, the coal was graded, washed and stored. The coal would then be taken on the MGR circuit to power stations in the Aire Valley - Eggborough, Drax and Ferrybridge.

Beforehand, it's worth putting Gascoigne Wood into perspective ....

The opening of the Aire Valley power stations became the focus for one of the most intensive freight operations, with around 300,000 tonnes of coal a week being take from around 30 collieries. In 1974, the Labour Government and National Coal Board (NCB), backed by the National Union of Mineworkers (NUM), initiated an ambitious expansion of coal production, named the 'Plan for Coal'. This involved maximising income from indigenous coal reserves, including the closure of older pits, and investment in new capacity, such as the Selby Coalfield.

The first coal emerged from Wistow mine, one of five constituent mines in the Selby complex, in July 1983. Apart from a lull during the 1984 miners' strike, coal production resumed in 1985 and, at its peak, more than 30 MGR trains would depart each day for the power stations. Most of the coal went to Drax (the largest coal fired power station in Europe) and during a working day, a single train could make four circuits!

Between 1995 and 1999, the operation turned from being successfully profitable to loss-making and by 2000, coal was no longer mined at two of the mines (Whitemoor and North Selby) and there was falling output from the other three mines. By 2000, the loss was £30 million per annum, resulting in UK Coal announcing the closure of the complex in 2002. The last coal train left Gascoigne Wood for Drax on 19th November 2004, bringing an end to one of Britain's most modern and highly-automated 'Superpits' - a decision that many experts believed to have been premature.

(above) : ***"Smoke gets in your Eyes"*** *.... well, in this case, exhaust fumes, as the driver looks back cautiously, while reversing No.56089 and a trainload of coal into Gascoigne Wood Up sidings, ready for departure time.*

(08/95)

(above) : *No.56089 is seen again, patiently waiting to depart Gascoigne Wood with a loaded MGR coal train.*

(below) : *Gascoigne Wood signal box, built in 1908 to a North Eastern Railway NE 24 design, had an electronic panel installed at the time of the development of Gascoigne Wood mine. The signal box controlled a 3-way junction, including connections to & from the Leeds - Hull main line, connecting curves north and south onto the York - Sheffield main line, plus a vast amount of sidings in the area. ((09/95)*

Waiting permission to proceed from the signalman, Loadhaul No.56077 waits to enter the Gascoigne Wood complex with an empty MGR. Note the signalman's white hatchback car parked alongside Milford Curve.

Burton Salmon

KNOTTINGLEY

Knottingley TMD is a Traction Maintenance Depot located in Knottingley, slightly east of Knottingley station on the south side of the Goole - Pontefract Baghill main line. It opened in 1967 to maintain the locos and MGR hopper wagons for a planned 75 Merry-go-Round trains a day operation, expected to fuel Drax, Eggborough and Ferrybridge power stations.

Whilst spending time at both Milford Junction and Knottingley station, I frequently observed a Class 08 shunting loco take a few HAA wagons from Milford West Sidings to the TMD for attention.

In 1976, Class 03, 04, 08 shunters and Class 47/3 locos could be seen at the depot and from the late 1970s until the 1990s, the depot being home to Class 56 locos.

When the depot opened in July 1967, it was coded 56A (previously used for a shed in Wakefield), before becoming 55G. Under TOPS, from 1973, it became simply 'KY'.

Selective Images:

(above) : *Seven of the eight cooling towers at Ferrybridge power station provide a fantastic backdrop for No.56011, which is taking the Up Doncaster line by the side of Knottingley TMD with empty HAA hoppers bound for stabling at Doncaster Decoy Reception Sidings. From there, the wagons will probably go to one of the Yorkshire 'super pits - Harworth, Maltby or Rossington for loading with yet more coal.*

(top left) : *Making a pleasant change from a procession of coal trains, No.56045 heads north in fading light with KIA steel carriers (fitted with a sliding roof), which form 6E31, the 12:54 Wolverhampton Steel Terminal - Lackenby. Behind the 'grid' are the Normanton lines, which go via Castleford and then through Healey Mills to reach the Calder Valley main line. MGR coal trains serving Ferrybridge power station go this way.*

(bottom left) : *Viewed through a 135mm lens, No.56100 heads along the Up Pontefract line and past the site of the old Burton Salmon railway station, which lasted until 1968 when all traffic ceased. The 'grid' will continue for another two miles as far as Ferrybridge North Junction, where it will take the spur to reach the Goole line at Knottingley West Junction, thence onwards to Eggborough / Drax power stations.* (07/95)

Sudforth Lane

(left) : *Loadhaul 'grid' No.56027 propels empty MGR hoppers in to Kellingley Colliery (the 'Big K') to be loaded with coal for Ferrybridge power station.*

Some coal from the 'Big K' went to Ferrybridge by barge on the adjacent Aire and Calder Navigation Canal.

My vantage point is by Sudforth Lane level crossing, controlled by a signal box, dating from 1959 in the BR era. It was originally equipped with a mechanical lever frame, which was later replaced with an electronic panel.

(middle) : *No.56088 heads east with a loaded MGR. Exploratory boreholes were sunk at Kellingley in the 1950s and coal production began in April 1965; along with Hatfield and Thoresby, it was one of the last three deep mines in the UK, closing in December 2015.*

(below) : ***"Lines of Power"***

Electricity transmission lines overpower No.56077 'Thorpe Marsh Power Station' as it approaches Sudforth Lane level crossing with a rake of empty HAA hoppers from either Eggborough or Drax, which had earlier brought in the coal to generate the power. *(09/95)*

Gilberdyke

(above) : *At this point, Loadhaul No.56118 joins the Hull and Selby Railway off the Hull and Doncaster branch of the North Eastern Railway, which opened in 1869 with 6D51, the 08:01 Doncaster Belmont - Hull 'Enterprise', comprising bogie bolster wagons laden with steel for Hedon Road steel terminal. The vantage point is Broad Lane road bridge, just west of Gilberdyke station, and below me on the right is (out of view) Gilberdyke signal box.*

November 2018, marked the end of traditional block signalling on the mainline to Hull with the closure of the signal boxes, including Gilberdyke, following control passing to York ROC. Three years earlier, the North Lincolnshire mainline through Barnetby experienced a similar fate when re-signalling handed over to York ROC. (07/01)

DONCASTER

(above) : *Doncaster station on the ECML was, and still is, a popular place where trainspotters congregate. Of course, not as busy now as in the 1980s when there was a regular flow of coal trains running to and from the Aire Valley power stations. Looking smart in its Loadhaul colours, No.56077 'Thorpe Marsh Power Station', proceeds along the Up Fast line at Doncaster with MGR empties.*

(below) : *Meanwhile, No.56084 'Selby Coalfield' makes its way through the station with MGR empties, while an unidentified ReS (Rail Express Systems) Class 47 waits at Platform 4 with 1V64, the 14:03 Low Fell - Plymouth mail, which would have been formed of five vans.*

(08/95)

(above) : *A unique train on the ECML sees the conveyance of concrete blocks from the Plasmor plant at Heck in purpose built PNA 2-axle open wagons. The plant is some 12 miles north of Doncaster, but can only be accessed from the Up Main of the ECML, which means the 'empties' are routed via Knottingley, Milford Junction and Hambleton Junctions to approach Heck from the north.*

Here, No.56085 crosses over onto the Down Fast line in order to reach Doncaster Decoy Yard where the train (6P68, the 16:50 Heck - Biggleswade) will recess overnight. *(08/95)*

(below) : *Looking south, Transrail liveried No.56007 is about to pass through Platform 4 road with an empty MGR heading for Gascoigne Wood, which presumably originated from either Cottam or West Burton power station.*

Knottingley (above) : *Rampart Lane Foot Crossing, two miles east of Knottingley station, was a great spot to see eastbound coal trains, especially in the morning when the sun was in the right aspect. Wisps of steam rise from the cooling towers at Ferrybridge power station as No.56094 'Eggborough Power Station', approaches the foot crossing with a loaded MGR.* (08/95)

Barnetby (above) : *I walked down a dirt track beside the running lines from Barnetby to Wrawby Junction and this was my reward. A fantastic array of semaphore signals, behind which is the equally as impressive signal box. Loadhaul No.56050 passes with empty steel carriers en-route to either grimsby Docks or Immingham.* (08/95)

(above) : *Trains of containerised Tioxide (red gypsum waste) were taken thrice-weekly to a landfill site at Roxby on the Flixborough branch (north of Scunthorpe) from the Tioxide works at Grimsby. Albeit a 'glinty' backlit shot, this is the only record I have of this working. No.56039 'Port of Hull' passes through Barnetby with 6D85, the 08:52 Grimsby - Roxby. Note the old yard lights in the sidings.* *(08/95)*

(opposite) : *This is a 'classic' shot taken from the footbridge at Barnetby station, looking west back towards Wrawby Junction. EWS liveried No.56069 passes through the station with 6G33, the 10:57 Eggborough p.s. - Lindsey empty fuel oil bogie tanks. Lindsey also provides fuel oil to Drax, Ferrybridge, Cottam and West Burton.*

(below) : *Another 'classic' Barnetby shot, with the semaphore signals the main attraction, although some might disagree, in view of a Loadhaul 'grid', No.56006, passing on the Up Slowline with an empty MGR, which is 6G05, the 12:39 Scunthorpe Steelworks - Immingham, running several hours early on this occasion.* *(08/95)*

BARNETBY

Barnetby railway station serves the village of Barnetby-le-Wold in North Lincolnshire. It is unstaffed and popular with railway enthusiasts due to the high volume of passing freight traffic.

Historically, the railway came to Barnetby in 1848 when the Great Grimsby and Sheffield Junction Railway was constructed linking:

Sheffield - Retford - Lincoln - Market Rasen - Barnetby - Grimsby

The most important connection, which is still the case today, was the Trent, Ancholme and Grimsby Railway in 1866, bringing the steel town of Scunthorpe into play. These railways became part of the Great Central Railway (GCR).

The GCR realised the importance of the Humber ports; Grimsby and the new Immingham Docks, unique in that a deep water channel made easy access for ships, irrespective of tides.

With increased traffic through Barnetby, the standard double track layout was deemed to be inadequate and resulted in the quadrupling of the track between Wrawby Junction and Brocklesby Junction. To handle the traffic, new signal boxes were built at Wrawby Junction, Barnetby West, Barnetby East, Melton Ross and Brocklesby Junction.

In 2001 a new footbridge (a hideous structure, some might say!) and the lines through the station were re-signalled over the Christmas and New Year of 2015/16, with new colour light signals installed and the old manual signal boxes at Wrawby Junction and Barnetby East closed.

Melton Ross

(left) : *EWS liveried No.56103 'Stora' passes the lime works at Melton Ross with 7H41, Immingham - Drax loaded MGR.*

Due to the relatively slow speed of this train, like many other freight trains, it was possible to take a photograph here and then drive to Scunthorpe for another photograph (see below), which is about the only time I have actually 'Chased a Train"!

This location is a precarious one, viewed from the A18 road bridge, which does not have a footpath on this side of the road; vehicles hurtle past unnervingly as they make their way to Grimsby - not for the faint-hearted!

(07/01)

Stainforth Junction

(opposite) : *Now that's what you call a goods train, in this case 6D65, Doncaster Belmont - Immingham 'Enterprise', headed by No.56103. You can count 10 different types of wagon in the consist, yet the track gang seem completely uninterested in the train's passing.*

Behind the rear wagons, out of view, a much used 'freight only' line leads to Applehurst Junction (for the ECML and Knottingley line) and to Skellow Junction (for Wakefield). *(07/00)*

Appleby Frodingham, Scunthorpe

(left) : *It is just under 15 miles and about 15 minutes to complete the car journey from Melton Ross to Scunthorpe.*

This vantage point is the A1029 Brigg Road bridge, which has a north west - south east orientation spanning the running lines at Appleby Frodingham, Scunthorpe, close to the steelworks.

The sidings on the left are to where MGR coal trains from Immingham to Scunthorpe run and then reverse to gain access into the Coal Handling Plant. Similarly, empty coal trains, returning to Immingham, have to do the same process.

Here, No.56103 is seen again passing through Scunthorpe with 7H41 for Drax. *(07/01)*

Out & About with "*STORA*"

56103

Number	:	56103	
Built	:	BREL Doncaster	
Introduced	:	December 1981	
First Allocation	:	Tinsley	
Named	:	September 1997	'Stora'
De-named	:	February 2006	
Fate	:	Withdrawn, November 2006	

Warrington Yard

(above) : *'Enterprise' wagonload freight services operated on a 'Hub and Spoke' system, with the yards at Wembley, Bescot, Warrington, Mossend, Doncaster and Newport being the major 'hubs', from which local 'trips' would serve terminals in each area.*

In this view, Loadhaul No.56074 'Kellingley Colliery' has arrived with 6M63, the 06:29 Mossend - Warrington Arpley 'Enterprise', where the OTA timber wagons are detached, going forward as 6J70, Arpley - Chirk 'trip'. (04/97)

Water Orton

(below) : *Water Orton, eight miles east of Birmingham New Street is a busy location, being a pinch point for north east - south west / south east / south Wales freight and traffic using the cross-country route linking Nuneaton and Bescot / Washwood Heath.*

Sadly, it is only an island platform with no ticket booking hall, nor refreshment or toilet facilities. However, the sheer volume of traffic compensates for its other shortcomings. This was a stop-over on my drive home to Swindon after spending an enjoyable day at Milford Junction.

(left) : *Coal sub-sector 'grid' No.56134 'Blyth Power' is about to pass through Water Orton, having reached here via the Sutton Park 'freight-only' line with 6E31, the 11:45 Wolverhampton Steel Terminal - Lackenby steel empties.*

The 'grid' is taking the Up Main line to Derby while the line on the far left is the Down Slow line. The other line is bi-directional taking 'Down' traffic off the Derby route and 'Up' traffic to Nuneaton. (09/95)

Going 'Dutch'

When British Rail operations were divided into sectors, a new version of Railfreight livery emerged giving sectors individual identities. Basically, a two-tone Grey livery was adopted, which included a logo on the bodyside to indicate which freight sector they belonged.

However, for locos used on internal British Rail duties, a separate livery of a plain darker grey was created, subsequently modified for locos allocated to the Civil Engineer's department, to include a yellow stripe on the upper bodyside. This livery became known as "Dutch" due to its similarity to the corporate colours of *Nederlandse Spoorwegen* and six Class 56s received this livery:

56031 / 56036 / 56046 / 56047 / 56048 / 56049

Wakefield

Calder Bridge Junction

(above) : *At the time of this visit, the area to the right of the running lines was completely overgrown, but was once the site of Wakefield Wagon Repair Depot, which I only ever visited once. This was on Sunday, 6th June 1976, when I came to see Class 03 No.03047, which was the fifth of a final 15 locos I needed to record seeing all 4,057 locos listed in my ian Allan Shedbook.*

I remembered the footbridge was at the end of a cul-de-sac, off the main A638 Wakefield to Doncaster road near Wakefield Trinity Rugby League Club. Looking north towards the crossover at Calder Bridge Junction, 'Dutch' Class 56 No.56049 approaches with 6E33, the10:57 Knowsley - Immingham 'Enterprise', the consist being mainly empty vans, which brought in newsprint for newspapers. *(08/03)*

Stenson Junction

(above) : *This was, and still is, a popular location where enthusiasts gather. Near the village of Findern, south of Derby, a lane off the A50 crosses the main Birmingham - Derby main line, which has good views of passing trains in both directions. The actual Stenson Junction is about 800-yards further north, where the 'freight-only' line to Sheet Stores Junction diverges right off the main line. I generally don't include light engine moves but for a Class 56 producing a lot of clag, I made an exception. No.56110 hurries north and you can see in the distance North Stafford Junction, where the line from Uttoxeter and Stoke-on-Trent joins the main line.* *(09/95)*

(below) : *Meanwhile, looking in the opposite direction, Loadhaul No.56109 decelerates towards North Stafford Junction, in order to leave the main line with a rake of empty bogie bolster wagons, which form 6M13, the 08:37 Tees Yard - Etruria.* *(09/95)*

"Fastline"

In May 2006, 'Fastline', a subsidiary of Jarvis, entered the railfreight market, initially with three Class 56s, each costing £700,000 to refurbish.

Based in Doncaster, their first working was an out & back intermodal between Doncaster Railport and Thamesport on the Isle of Grain.

The train was frequently poorly loaded and became known as the 'Fresh Air Express'. Although loadings did improve, the Company ceased trading in March 2010.

(right) : *A very lightly loaded 4O90, the 10:51 Doncaster Railport - Thamesport passes Stenson Junction with a payload of three containers, hauled by No.56302, which was No.56124 in a previous life.* (06/06)

(below) : *This intermodal was booked for a crew change at Rugby (16:25hrs) and No.56301 (ex.No.56045) waits at Signal RY92 on the Up Goods line for its new driver.* (09/06)

6M47

Aldwarke - Wolverhampton

Burton-on-Trent

(right) : *During 2002, I was out & about quite a lot during the summer months looking for suitable photographs for use on the front covers of various publications on which I was working at that time.*

One of my key targets was 6M47, the 08:55 Aldwarke - Wolverhampton Steel Terminal, basically because it was an interesting commodity (steel products) and pretty well guaranteed for Class 56 traction.

All I had to do was select a location which lent itself to a 'portrait-style' photograph.

Here, EWS No.56094 'Eggborough Power Station' hurries through Burton on Trent with 6M47, consisting of bogie bolster wagons containing steel bars and rods.

Kingsbury

(opposite) : *This was a popular location of mine, Kingsbury on the Birmingham - Derby main line, which afforded great views of southbound freight in the morning and afternoon, plus the bonus of viewing petroleum tanks serving the nearby oil terminal.*

Loadhaul, 'grid' No.56118 passes the spot; the vantage point being Trinity Road bridge, accessed off the Main A51 in the village of Kingsbury.

Whitacre junction

(right) : *After passing Kingsbury, 6M47 could be routed to Water Orton by either the direct route via Lea Marston or via Whitacre Junction. I simply had to make a choice of where to place myself.*

I invariably opted for Whitacre Junction on the Birmingham - Water Orton - nuneaton main line.

No.56090 has swept into view with 6M47 and this photo. became the front cover of Freightmaster No.90, with the Burton on Trent photo. of No.56094 on the back cover.

The lines to the left lead to Kingsbury Junction and the ones to the right lead to Nuneaton.

'Grids' on the Western

Didcot East

(above) : *The Class 56s used to work MGR coal trains to Didcot power station in the early '80s, plus stone trains originating from Merehead and Whatley, plus Tytherington. Otherwise, the 56s have not been regular performers in my neck of the woods. Most sightings were by exception, as illustrated on this page.*

Loadhaul 'grid' No.5611 approaches a red signal at Didcot East Junction with a short train of containers, forming 6V38, the 09:02 Marchwood - Didcot Yard MoD stores, a Class 58 turn at the time.

(09/02)

Oxford

(left) : *Another Loadhaul 'grid', this time No.56027, passes Hinksey, Oxford, just like the good old days with a loaded MGR train, albeit this one is going north.*

Running in the path of 6M14, Avonmouth - Rugby coal, the MEAs have been swapped for HAAs to form 6M14 to Ironbridge power station on this particular day. *(05/98)*

Cardiff Pengam

(above) : *This image was taken before Cardiff freightliner terminal at Pengam closed and the new Wentloog terminal opened three miles further east. The site has since been completely demolished and, you've guessed, developed for residential housing.*

At the time this photograph was taken, although MGR coal trains were in the hands of Class 56s, EWS hired in two Class 59s to work the Port Talbot Docks - Llanwern iron ore trains, before Class 60s took over.

Two-tone grey Class 56 no.56054 'British Steel Llanwern' passes Pengam freightliner terminal with 6B653, the16:53 Llanwern - Port Talbot Grange Sidings HAA empties. In the terminal, Class 47s Nos.47301 + 47150 drop onto 4S81 to Coatbridge and No.47301 waits to work 4L56 to Felixstowe.

The vantage point for this photograph is the railway overbridge on Rover Way, which leads from the A469 into Tremorfa and Cardiff Docks. *(05/98)*

Kings Sutton

(above) : *"It's a fix" ..... a train most well known for 'dropping' rare traction at the time was 1V96, the 09:10 Edinburgh Waverley - Reading. Although 'booked' for a Class 47/8 loco forward from Birmingham New Street, this loco was often used to cover loco shortages / failures, leaving this duty uncovered. On Friday, 15th May 1998, with just a week to go before the end of the winter timetable,, the sole BR Blue 'grid' made a surprise appearance on the train.*

The 'grid', No.56004, is seen here working the return 1M79, the 16:47 Reading - Liverpool Lime Street past the idyllic rural backdrop of Kings Sutton, south of Banbury. *(05/98)*

Class 56s Fleet Survey 1st April 2020

COLAS

No.	Pool	Location	Working
56049	COFS	Doncaster Up Yard	
56051	COFS	Nottingham CMD	
56078	COFS	Grangemouth Oil Terminal	0Z56, Grangemouth Oil Terminal - Millerhill
56087	COFS	Barnetby	0Y69, Barnetby - Eastleigh
56090	COFS	Barnetby	0Y69, Barnetby - Eastleigh
56094	COFS	Nottingham CMD	
56096	COFS	Barnetby	0Y69, Barnetby - Eastleigh
56105	COFS	Cardiff Canton TMD	
56113	COFS	Eastcroft	
56302	COFS	Barnetby	0Z02, Barnetby - Doncaster

GBRf

No.	Pool	Location	Working
56031	GBGS	Longport	
56032	GBGS	Longport	
56037	GBGS	Longport	
56069	GBGS	Longport	
56081	GBGD	Peak Forest	
56098	GBGD	Leicester SD	
56311	GBGS	Longport	
56312	GBGD	Peak Forest	

DCR

No.	Pool	Location	Working
56091	HTLX	Willesden DCR	
56103	HTLX	Willesden DCR	
56303	HTLX	Willesden DCR	

UK RAIL LEASING

No.	Pool	Location	Working
56007	UKRS	Longport	
56018	UKRS	Longport	
56038	UKRS	Longport	
56060	UKRS	Longport	
56065	UKRS	Longport	
56077	UKRS	Longport	
56104	UKRL	Leicester SD	
56106	UKRS	Leicester SD	
56301	UKRL	Carlisle Kingmoor Yard	

(above) : *EWS maroon & gold livery Class 60 No.60053 'Nordic Terminal' passes Stenson Junction, a well known railway hotspot for photographers on the Birmingham - Derby main line, with a trainload of steel slab, running as 6V36, Lackenby - Llanwern.*

The lines deviating off the main line to the right (near the rear of the train) lead onto the 'freight only' line, which runs to Sheet Stores Junction to join the Midland Main Line, with routes to Toton, Nottingham or south to Loughborough.

No.60053 was originally named 'John Reith', but was renamed 'Nordic Terminal' at Thornaby in February 1997 to twin with an EWS customer.

(04/02)

'Tugs'

Setting The Scene

In the 1980s, British Rail identified the need for a high-powered Type 5 diesel loco for use on its Trainload Freight sector, capable of hauling very heavy trains around Britain's railways at a maximum of 60mph. Consequently, after competitive tendering, Brush Traction in Loughborough were chosen to build 100 of these locos, which would become:

Class 60s - Nos.60001 - 60100 Built between 1989 - 1993

Enthusiasts nicknamed them 'tugs', presumably just like a naval tug they can move an incredible load!

Names

In 1989, in traditional fashion, Railfreight named the Class 60s, based on their respective freight sector. Principally;

- Construction and Metals : British mountains.
- Coal and petroleum : Famous British citizens, with an emphasis on science and engineering.

There were exceptions; No.60001 'Steadfast' and No.60098 'Charles Francis Brush'.

Decline

With the arrival of the dreaded Class 66/0 'sheds' from the late 1990s, this marked the end for many 'tugs', especially due to their poor reliability, which was not helped by a lack of maintenance. To give you an idea of the decline, here are a few figures showing the number of 'tugs' in traffic:

May 2007	60 'tugs'	half the fleet!
Jan 2010	5	60009 / 60049 / 60059 / 60071 / 60096
Jan 2011	6	60010 / 60015 / 60040 / 60045 / 60074 / 60099

Super 'Tugs'

A saving grace came in January 2011, when DB Schenker announced a plan to refurbish and upgrade a total of 21 Class 60s - *'Super Tugs'* - to improve reliability and extend the working life of each loco by 15 years.

After trying to get rid of these locos DBS realised, probably reluctantly, that there was a need to have 60s to haul the very heavy trains (eg. block loads of stone, petroleum, etc) as the 66s were not up to the task. They even trialled pairs of Class 66s on heavy stone trains out of Peak Forest, coal trains out of Liverpool Gladstone Dock and Robeston petroleum trains, all to no avail.

No.60007 became the first 'Super 60' to be overhauled.

First Impressions

I first caught sight of a Class 60 during a visit to Barnetby in August 1995 and I must say, I was not impressed, I did'na like 'em! The design just looked like a rectangular box on wheels, unlike the Class 50s and 56s, which were more aesthetically pleasing on the eye. Of course, the good old days of diesel locos having a nose, like that of the 37s, 40s and 'Peaks', had regrettably, long gone.

However, as we moved into the 2000s, I did grow to like them, probably helped in no small part that 'sheds' were replacing traditional classes of loco - 31, 33s, 37s, 47s, 56s, 58s, etc.

So, with this in mind, I have assembled a collection of some of my favourite images of Class 60s at work around the network.

60007

(above) : *This image was the first photograph I took with a digital SLR (Single Lens Reflex) camera, which also coincided with my first visit to Elford, a popular location among photographers, three miles north of Tamworth on the Birmingham - Derby main line. With a backdrop of oil seed rape in full bloom, Loadhaul Class 60 No.60007 passes with 6M57, Lindsey - Kingsbury loaded petroleum tanks.* *(06/04)*

(below) : *In October 1994, Transrail launch 'Enterprise' and Warrington (Arpley) became the 'central hub' of the new system, where trains arrive to attach/detach wagons. From there, 'trips' will serve other terminals in the vicinity. In this view, No.60007 is seen again, this time accelerating out of Warrington Yard, with 6J70, Warrington - Chirk, conveying timber on OTA wagons off the overnight 6M63, Mossend - Warrington.* *(04/97)*

60081 'Isambard Kingdom Brunel'
"The 'tug' that Got Away"

(above) : *One of the most celebrated Class 60 repaints took place in August 2000, when EWS repainted No.60081 into a mock Great Western Railway lined green livery and applied cast iron nameplates 'Isambard Kingdom Brunel'. Here, approaching Highworth Junction, Swindon, No.60081 is in charge of a loaded rake of the iconic HAA, 2-axle, coal wagons which forms 6A65, the 08:51 Avonmouth Bulk Import terminal - Didcot power station.*

Sadly, the loco suffered a major power unit failure in early 2005 and was withdrawn from service, now languishing in a long line of Class 60s at Toton, in store, probably awaiting the cutter's torch. It is criminal that such a unique loco was not saved for posterity and displayed at the National Rail Museum in York. (07/01)

60006

This particular 'tug' has the unenviable distinction of being the first Class 60 to be scrapped; by Ron Hull Ltd at Toton in 2020.

Along with No.60033, this loco received Corus silver grey livery in 2000, the corporate colours of British Steel's successor.

Previously, in July 1997, It was named 'Scunthorpe Steelmaster', the same time as it also received blue livery. It was originally named 'Great Gable' when new.

(left) : *An appropriate working for No.60006 'Scunthorpe Steelmaster'.*

The 'doll' has been set to indicate that No.60006 will pass through Barnetby on the Down Slow line with 6T27, Immingham - Santon and JTA/JUA tipplers filled with iron ore for Scunthorpe steelworks.

The semaphores at Barnetby were a great sight until they were replaced by MAS colour lights in December 2015.

RIP No.60006.

(Above) : *With the power station providing the backdrop, a Pendolino speeds south en route to London Euston, as the silver-grey machine trundles along the Down Slow line at Rugeley Trent Valley with 6H55, Bletchley - Peak Forest empties. Note, the first three wagons are the three distinctive designs in this JGA category.* (07/04)

"All Lines Lead to Scunthorpe"

(above) : *The A1029 road bridge which spans the main line at Frodingham, Scunthorpe, is a great vantage point and a busy scene afforded to me at the time of my visit. Three trains in view, which are, from left to right:*

No.56060	*7C79,*	*Scunthorpe Steelworks - Immingham*	*empty MGR*	
No.56103	*7H41,*	*Immingham - Milford*	*loaded MGR coal*	
No.60018	*6M06,*	*Roxby - Bredbury*	*empty GMC 'Binliner'*	*(07/01)*

(above) : *The closure of the Allied Steel & Wire plant at Tremorfa, Cardiff, in July 2002, resulted in a complete revamp of scrap metal services with several being withdrawn completely. One casualty of the ASW closure was the loss of 6V99, the (FO) Hamworthy - Cardiff Tidal scrap train.*

With two cooling towers at Didcot power station dominating the background, 6V99 passes Milton on the Down Goods line with No.60022 hauling the train. The consist is some SSA 2-axle open scrap wagons and a mix of JNA bogie scrap wagons, which would be in the series GERS 4400 - 4425 and TIPH 9800 9835; the latter being the ones with a bar towards the top of the wagon. *(05/02)*

(above) : *Transrail Class 60 No.60061 approaches Hatfield & Stainforth with 6D66, Immingham - Doncaster 'Enterprise'. The loco was new in April 1991 when it was named 'Alexander Graham Bell 1847 - 1922', the inventor of the telephone but, as you can see, the loco had lost its nameplate by the time this photo was taken. (08/04)*

(below) : *Prior to EWS maroon & gold livery, EWS (English, Scottish & Welsh Railway) applied its 'Beasties' logo to the bodyside, consisting of three heads: the lion of England, the dragon of Wales and the stag of Scotland.*

Two-tone grey 'tug' No.60091 'An Teallach' arrives at Didcot yard with 6O26, Hinksey Yard - Eastleigh with a consist of JNA 'Falcon' Network Rail bogie ballast wagons. This train has been running for many, many years and after the EWS era it was operated by Freightliner Heavy Haul and, currently, Colas Rail. (05/07)

Construction Materials (top left) : *Inappropriate for this train, No.60057 'Adam Smith' sports 'Coal Sector' decals but, in practice, locos frequently interchanged between freight flows. No.60057 is seen passing Washwood Heath, Birmingham, with a rake of MBA 'Monster' bogie box wagons loaded with stone, running as 6M29, Peak Forest - Brierley Hill.* *(10/02)*

(top right) : *No.60036 'GEFCO' heads through Courtenhall cutting on the 'Northampton Loop Line' with 6B10, Peak Forest - Bletchley loaded stone in RMC bogie hoppers. Note, the PCA 2-axle cement powder tanks in the consist.* *(07/05)*

Departmental (below) : *The footbridge at Millbrook station, Southampton, is a good vantage point to view freight traffic, in both directions, actually. EWS liveried No.60049 approaches the station with a long rake of wagons, which include some 2-axle open wagons and long welded rail carriers, running as 6O41, Westbury Yard - Eastleigh. Millbrook Freightliner terminal is In the background, where Class 47 No.47279 is in attendance.* *(07/03)*

Minerals - Iron Ore (above) : Looking towards Wrawby Jct., *Loadhaul 'tug' No.60038 enters Barnetby station with 6K22, Santon - Immingham empty iron ore tipplers; the steelworks at Scunthorpe consumes vast tonnages of both iron ore and coal in the steel production process.* *(07/01)*

MGR Coal (above) : *No.60057 'Adam Smith' passes Whitacre Junction with a loaded MGR which, according to my notes, forms 7T52, Hicks Lodge - Daw Mill, a service which takes coal to Daw Mill for blending. This train reversed at Washwood Heath to gain access to the Nuneaton line.* *(04/02)*

Domestic Waste (below) : *The GMC (Greater Manchester Council) 'Binliners' were a solid 'tug' turn working to a landfill site at Roxby, near Scunthorpe. Here, No.60020 heads through Oakenshaw with 6E06, Bredbury - Roxby.* *(07/06)*

'Enterprise' (below) : *A favourite image - Mainline Blue No.60044 crosses the River Don Navigation at Kirk Sandall with the daily 6D65, Doncaster - Immingham 'Enterprise', formed mainly of steel carrying wagons.* *(06/04)*

Petroleum Products (top left) : *A cracking vantage point .... viewed from a footpath overlooking Narroways Hill Junction, Bristol, EWS-liveried No.60049 heads 6V13, Furzebrook - Hallen Marsh 2-axle LPG) Liquefied Petroleum Gas tanks. (08/97)*

(top right) : *Another favourite place for railway photographers is Greenhome, near Tebay on the WCML, where we see No.60047 heading south with 6M19, Jarrow - Stanlow 2-axle petroleum tank empties. Oil traffic over Shap ended in January 1998. (04/97)*

(below) : *No.60054 'Charles Babbage' slowly heads along the Down Goods line at Pilning with 6B33, Theale - Robeston empty bogie tanks. Murco introduced the new red liveried TEA petroleum tanks in January 2002. (06/03)*

(below) : *A superb collection of semaphore signals control the eastern approach to Barnetby station, seen in this view of EWS 'beasties' No.60070 about to enter the station with loaded petroleum tanks, forming 6M06, Lindsey - Kingsbury. (07/06)*

Metals (top left) : *Two-tone grey 'tug' with Loadhaul logo, No.60064 'Back Tor' is a fine sight as it crosses the South Wales main line on Bishton Flyover at Llandevenny with 6M96, Llanwern - Corby loaded steel coil, which normally originates from Margam.*

The Up Relief line snakes over the main line from Llanwern and descends an incline to run parallel with the Up Main line. Interestingly, the Down relief line stays on the level, which can be seen deviating off to the left. This location has proved to be a popular vantage point amongst photographers, although the view in the opposite direction is less appealing. (06/03)

(below) : *No.60014 'Alexander Fleming' is in charge of 6V37, Lackenby - Llanwern loaded steel slabs, which is seen snaking across the points at Milford junction. The loco sports petroleum sector yellow & blue waves logo.* (03/03)

(below) : *EWS maroon & gold 'tug', No.60010, approaches Hatfield & Stainforth station with 6N30, Scunthorpe - Lackenby steel slabs. At the time, Hatfield Mine was still operational and formed a great backdrop.* (07/00)

(left) : *Poor light seems to beset me during photographic trips in high-summer (July and August), convincing me that I would be better off going out during the spring and autumn.*

At Barnetby, I was looking forward to seeing and photographing my first Colas 'tug' but, with rapidly fading light, my shot was not what I had hoped for.

Nevertheless, after driving for nearly four hours and some 200 miles, I wasn't going home empty-handed!

After a brief rain squall as well, No.60076 'Dunbar' arrived with 6E82, the 12:16 Rectory Junction - Lindsey discharged petroleum tanks. (07/15)

Lindsey oil refinery on South Humberside sees black & orange for the first time since the demise of Loadhaul, as Colas Rail develop their share of the petro-chemical market, serving Colnbrook (6V70), Preston Docks (6M32) and Rectory Junction (6M11). This gain from DBS is, perhaps, not surprising as the trains run on behalf of TOTAL, a French-owned company, as is Colas Rail.

The previous year - 2014 - Colas Rail replaced DBS as traction provider for a service of export steel from Llanwern Steelworks to the Port of Tilbury. I was keen to snap a Colas 'tug' fot the first time.

(below) : *A backdrop of Didcot power station at Steventon, is no longer possible following the closure of the coal fired-power station and the resultant demolition of the cooling towers and chimney stack. In this view, No.60087 'CLIC Sargeant' approaches the B4017 road bridge with a fine assortment of steel carriers, which form 6V62, the 11:12 Tilbury - Llanwern. This loco seemed to be ever-present on this particular flow!* (09/14)

Westerleigh Tanks

"Heavens Above" .... a mere 30 minutes separate these two images taken at Gloucester and demonstrate the vagary of our climate - one minute the sun is shining brightly, then the heavens open, the sky darkens and torrential rain falls, only for sunshine to return as quickly as it left.

(above) : *A DB Schenker cherry red 'tug' No.60007 'The Spirit of Tom Kendell' ascends the brief 1 in 178 incline into Gloucester station with 6B13, the 05:00 Robeston - Westerleigh loaded petroleum tanks. Note there are five different designs of bogie tank in the consist!*

(below) : *It's so dark, the red colour light signals positively gleam, as No.60054 passes through Gloucester with 6B41, the 11;34hrs discharged tanks returning from Westerleigh oil terminal to Robeston. An ISO speed rating of 800 was needed to capture this service - hope you think it was worth it!* *(09/16)*

DB
60007

60040

6B33

(above) : **60084** *has emerged from the west portal of Patchway Short Tunnel (62 yards long) with 6B33, Theale - Robeston empty bogie tanks. Note, the 60 does not have its number displayed on the front cab and that the 'Up' tunnel is at a lower level, known as Patchway New Tunnel, a mere 1,760 yards long.* *(05/06)*

(top left) : **60096** *is seen on an embankment above a field of oil seed rape at Knighton, on the Great Western Main Line in the Vale of the White Horse. This image may seem insignificant, but it is rather poignant to me, as when my mother spent some time in a residential care home, she very much liked to have a drive out in my car and see the trains. This was a popular spot for us both. Happy memories!*

(opposite, middle) : **60007** *'The Spirit of Tom Kendell' became the first 'Super Tug' to be overhauled following DB Schenker's decision to refurbish and upgrade 21 Class 60s. The refurbished machine, looking extremely smart in its new cherry red livery, approaches Highworth Junction, Swindon, heading 6B33 towards a pathing stop in Swindon East Loop.*

(bottom left) : ***60040*** *was named 'The Territorial Army Centenary' on 14th June 2008 at the National Rail Museum (York) by HRH The Prince Andrew, to mark the centenary of the Territorial Army. The loco was painted maroon for the event.*

The 'tug' is seen crawling towards a stop at a red signal on the Down Relief line at Challow with a rake of old TDA / TEA bogie tanks. This image, along with the other three, was before new red-liveried TEA tanks built by Wagony Swidnica, Poland, came on stream. *(08/08)*

(above) : **No.60021** Carlisle Citadel (07/16)

Class 60s Fleet Survey 1st April 2020

No.	Pool	Location	Working
DB CARGO			
60001	WCAT	Immingham TMD	6M99, Immingham - Wolverhampton Steel Term.
60007	WCBT	Toton TMD	
60010	WCBT	Doncaster Belmont	
60011	WCAT	Toton TMD	
60015	WCBT	Bescot	6E02, Bescot - Boston Docks
60017	WCBT	Peak Forest	6F05, Tunstead - Lostock Works
60019	WCAT	Warrington Arpley	
60020	WCBT	Toton TMD	
60024	WCAT	Tees Yard	
60039	WCAT	Toton TMD	
60040	WCAT	Redcar	6N03, Redcar - Scunthorpe Steelworks
60044	WCAT	Margam TC	6A11, Robeston - Theale
60054	WCBT	Robeston	6B13, Robeston - Westerleigh
60059	WCBT	Rotherham Steel Terminal	6D94, Rotherham Steel Term. - Hull Hedon Road
60062	WCAT	Lindsey Oil Refinery	6M57, Lindsey - Kingsbury
60063	WCAT	Margam TC	
60065	WCAT	Toton TMD	
60066	WCAT	Toton TMD	
60074	WCAT	Toton TMD	
60091	WCBT	Immingham TMD	
60092	WCBT	Toton TMD	
60100	WCAT	Toton TMD	
GBRf			
60002	GBTG	Toton TMD	
60021	GBTG	Tuebrook Sidings	
60026	GBTG	Doncaster Belmont	
60047	GBTG	Lynemouth p.s.	6N83, Lynemouth - Tyne Dock
60056	GBTG	Drax p.s.	6N20, Drax p.s. - Tyne Dock
60076	GBTG	Hexthorpe, Doncaster	
60085	GBTG	Tuebrook Sidings	
60087	GBTG	Toton TMD	
60095	GBTG	Toton TMD	
60096	GBTG	Drax p.s.	6M34, Drax - Tuebrook Sidings
DCR			
60028	HTLX	Willesden DCR	
60029	HTLX	Toton TMD	
60046	HTLX	Carlisle Kingmoor Yard	
60055	HTLX	Willesden DCR	6Z93, Willesden DCR - Westbury yard

(overleaf) *: I appreciate it may seem that images of 6B33 'Murco Tanks' have been a trifle excessive but, as it is the only source of regular Class 60 traction on the GWML, it does provide some great photographic opportunities, I hope you will forgive my indulgence with this particular train.*

(Page 72) *: A farm track off the South Moreton to Cholsey road, bisecting Manor Farm, leads to a railway bridge which, prior to electrification of the GWML, was a popular spot to watch and photograph the trains. I chose this particular vista from the south side of the railway to include the village church, as No.60062 was about to pass. St. Mary's church was founded as an abbey church by King Ethelred the Unready in approximately 986, rebuilt between 1150 - 1170, but retained its original cruciform shape. (09/13)*

(Page 73) *: During 2016, engineering work in Severn Tunnel saw several freight services diverted from Swindon via Kemble, Gloucester and Chepstow, before rejoining the South Wales main line at Severn Tunnel Junction. No.60007 'The Spirit of Tom Kendell' has passed through the 409 yards Kemble Tunnel on the approach to Kemble station with the diverted 6B33 to Robeston. (09/16)*

MURCO
DB SCHENKER

10
SW
1334
100
25
Passengers must not pass this point or cross the line
Warning
Do not trespass on the Railway
Penalty £1000
Trains run either way on this line

NEWPORT (Casnewydd)

Setting The Scene

In the 1970s, I well remember my father saying to me ***"Why go all over the country to see trains, when Newport is as busy and it's nearer to home"***.

In the 1980s, I did exactly that and soon realised the merit of his statement - as I stood on Platform 2 at Newport station, the colour light signals on both the Up Relief and the Down Relief lines were constantly changing from 'Red' to 'Green', again and again, as a procession of freight trains passed me by.

It is worth putting this scenario into context because, unlike today, there were many factors:

- Severn Tunnel marshalling yard was still open.
- Llanwern steelworks still had operational blast furnaces to make steel.
- South Wales coal mines generated trainloads of coal.
- Port Talbot/Margam sent regular trains of coal and iron ore to Llanwern steelworks.
- Ebbw Vale tinplate plant still operational.

Today, all the above are no more, save that Llanwern still rolls out steel products, although the blast furnaces have long gone.

Newport Station

(above) : *Ex-works Transrail Class 56, No.56066, is seen about to pass through Newport station on the Down Relief line with 6B57, the 13:15 Llanwern - Margam empty MGR coal hoppers.* *(11/95)*

East Usk

(right) : *The bodyside of this Mainline liveried Class 60 has been defaced by the application of a EWS 'Beasties' logo although, in fairness, the loco looks as if it could do with a lick of paint.*

It is passing East Usk on the Up Relief line with 6M41, Margam - Round Oak loaded steel. *(08/06)*

The Locations

East Usk

On a day out to Newport, East Usk was always my first port of call, mainly to view eastbound freight en-route to Llanwern steelworks, coal and iron ore trains, in particular. It was an easy drive for me to Newport, just over an hour, via the M4 motorway, leaving at Junction 24 to take the B4237, then onto Somerton Road where the road crosses the line about half-a-mile later. I parked the car in a side road to the north of the railway.

A pavement crossed the bridge for pedestrians, from where I could stand safely and photograph eastbound trains. However, on the other side, there was no path, and I had to stand by the side of the road to photograph westbound trains in the afternoon - a risky business, as this was a very busy road, not recommended, and I frequently moved back and forth for safety. At least the MAS signals gave me adequate warning of approaching freight trains.

On one unfortunate occasion, whilst on the wrong side of the bridge, so to speak, a passing car sounded its horn and a man hurled a mouthful of abuse at me, taking me by surprise and I dropped my camera on to the track below. Remarkably, there were only a few dents and scratches, but it still worked; a passing Permanent Way gang spotted it and one of the gang kindly brough it up to me.

Semaphore signalling was still present and operational at East Usk, solely to control access to and from the Uskmouth branch. The semaphore signals were subsequently removed when the line was re-signalled and arsonists struck in the dead of night on 19th April 2009, rendering East Usk signal box to a burnt-out shell.

Newport Station

The station here originally opened in 1850 as Newport High Street by the South Wales Railway Company and was greatly expanded in 1928; the suffix High Street became unnecessary on the closure of Mill Street and Dock Street stations to goods traffic in the 1960s

April 1961 saw the introduction of Multiple-Aspect colour light signalling (MAS) and with it modifications to the station layout. Ostensibly, the station became an island platform (Platforms 2 and 3) with through running lines to the south of this platform. The old Platform 8 became the new Platform 1, where the main station buildings are located, accessed from Queensway.

The platform ends provided great vantage points to watch and photograph all passing freight with unrestricted views in both directions. In terms of the position of the sun, mornings were best looking west and looking east in the afternoon, both vistas from Platform 1.

To the west of the station, Godfrey Road stabling point was located and there were usually a good number of Class 37s stabled, before the stabling of locos moved to ADJ yard. Further on, the railway plunges into Hillfield Tunnels, which were dug under Stow Hill in the 1840s.

Alexandra Dock Junction

The busy yard at Alexandra Dock Junction lies to the west of Newport station, on the 'Down' side of the South Wales main line, running in a north-south direction at this point. The yard's main functions are to serve rail-borne traffic at Newport Docks and to act as the main hub for engineering traffic in South Wales.

Locationally speaking, the yard is bounded by the B4237 road to the north and the A48 at the south end. In fact, there is a McDonalds restaurant beside the B4237, which not only provided me with light refreshment but a good vantage point at the rear of the building to observe northbound trains.

At the other end of the yard, off the B4237, Maesglas Avenue led to a lane which crossed the south end of the yard, which gave the best views of all, albeit southbound services only. Plus, I could park the car on the bridge itself, so it was always in safe view

In fact, there was never a dull moment here, as well as the trains, there was the spectacle of youths crossing the lines, laden with boxes of goods stolen from the nearby supermarket.

East Usk

At this time, East Usk Yard was still heavily used, mainly to stage MGR coal trains awaiting a path or for handling South Wales 'Speedlink' services.

The 'Speedlink' association arose from railfreight's decision to close Severn Tunnel Junction marshalling yard. Consequently, from November 1987, wagonload freight was diverted to other yards, East Usk would handle South wales 'Speedlink' wagons along with Cardiff Tidal.

The writing was on the wall for STJ, dating back to when the 'Up' and 'Down' shunting humps closed in 1978 and 1980, respectively.

(left) : *Coal sector Class 37/8 No.37894 heads east with a short rake of 2-axle open wagons loaded with ballast, which forms 7C40, the 12:06 Newport ADJ - Exeter Riverside. The semaphore signal controls access on to the Up Uskmouth branch.* *(01/97)*

(below) : *EWS maroon & gold Class 60 No.60097 'Port of Grimsby & Immingham' + Mainline two-tone grey No.60073 approach East Usk with 6V75, Dee Marsh - Margam, running via Llanwern, to detach / attach wagons.* *(09/03)*

(above) : *Class 60 No.60082, having left the stabling point at Godfrey Road, Newport, is seen running light engine (0M41) past East Usk signal box to work 6M41, Llanwern - Round Oak. This service normally runs direct from Margam.*

The signal box and sidings are clearly visible; an EWS Class 66/0 ('shed') is waiting to leave the yard with 4C58, the 13:13 East Usk - Avonmouth empty MGR coal hoppers. (05/06)

(right) : *During my visits to Newport, MGR coal trains to Llanwern steelworks were in the hands of single Transrail Class 56s, whilst the iron ore trains were worked double-headed by Class 56s, both being a wonderful sight.*

In hazy light, No.56053 'County of Mid-Glamorgan' ambles along the Up Relief line with 6B54, the12:52 Margam - Llanwern loaded MGR coal train. It will shortly leave the main line at Llanwern West Junction for the steelworks.

At the time, the majority of coal hoppers on this MGR-style circuit were fitted with 'hoods' and based at Barry. (01/97)

(**Overleaf**) : *A splendid sight .... a pair of Railfreight Grey, large logo, 'Grids', No.56050 + No.56043 approach East Usk with 6Z43, the 16:45 Llanwern - Port Talbot Docks empty iron ore tipplers.* (10/86)

NEWPORT STATION

(left) : *Class 37 No.37147 ambles along the Down Main with 7A62, the 14:55 Severn Tunnel Junction - Machen Quarry empty 2-axle ballast empties. It had been a foggy day and the mist had just about lifted in time for the first photograph of the day.*

(middle) : *Is this the type of duty intended for a Class 37/4 equipped with Electric Train Heating? Probably not, but if there is no passenger work, the loco may as well be put to good use instead of sitting idle on the depot.*

No.37427 'Bont Y Bermo' ambles through Newport with loaded mineral wagons, which forms 7A67, the 11:40 Oakdale - East Usk.

As No.D6988 when delivered in June 1965, it became No.37288 under TOPS, before its ETH conversion in February 1986, when it became No.37427.

(below) : *Still in original BR Blue livery, Class 56 No.56052 passes through the Platform 2 road with 6C08, the 13:30 Langley - Robeston discharged TDA bogie petroleum tanks.* *(All 10/86)*

(Previous Page) : *A fabulous setting, the view looking east from the multi-story car park near Newport railway station. Transrail Class 60 No.60082 'Mam Tor' heads across River Usk Viaduct with a trainload of steel coil, forming 6V75, Dee Marsh - Margam, made up BLA steel coil wagons.*

In the foreground is part of the ruined Newport Castle, a garrison, built in the 14th century, by either Hugh de Audley, 1st Earl of Gloucester or his son-in-law, Ralph, Earl of Stafford, for the purpose of managing the crossing of the River Usk. In 1402 it was sacked by Owain Glyndŵr and later taken by Oliver Cromwell's forces in 1648 during the Civil War. Its use declined further and was in a state of ruin by 1743. (09/02)

(above) : *'An interloper' .... Class 50s were not an everyday sight in the Principality. Here, deputising for a Class 47, No.50043 'Eagle' gets underway after making the Newport station stop with empty vans from Cardiff to Old Oak Common. No.50043 was named 'Eagle' in June 1978 after a Royal Navy aircraft carrier.* *(05/87)*

(below) : *It was pleasing to see another livery, other than the ubiquitous BR Blue, which so many locos carried. As part of sectorisation, locos carried decals on the bodyside to signify the sector to which they were allocated. In this case, black diamonds on a yellow background, denotes the coal sector, and No.37895 is in charge of 6V07, the 09:50 Seaforth - Gwaun Cae Gurwen 'Cawoods' containerised coal empties.* *(06/95)*

Iron Ore 'Grids'

(above) : *Pairs of Class 56s were used on the heavy Port Talbot to Llanwern iron ore trains from 1979, taking over from triple headed Class 37s; the 56s in turn gave way to double-headed Class37/7s and, finally, to a single Class 60. Railfreight Grey Large Logo No56043 + BR Blue No.56040 'Oystermouth' are seen in charge of 6C48, the 14:45 Llanwern - Port Talbot Docks empty tipplers.*

(below) : *The same pair are seen again, with No.56040 leading this time, on a loaded train of iron ore, which is 7C52, the 10:55 Port Talbot Docks - Llanwern. These Type 5 heavyweights were certainly a stirring sight.*

(above) : *BR Blue Nos.56001 + 56032 'County of South Glamorgan' make their approach with 6C41, the 12:05 Llanwern - Port Talbot Docks. No.56001, the doyen member of the Class, was built by Electroputere, Romania, introduced in February 1977, allocated to Tinsley MPD. It was withdrawn in September 1996.*

(below) : *At the west end of Newport station, Nos.56043 + 56050 are seen working another 7C52 trainload of iron ore. These trains, along with MGR coal to Llanwern, stopped running when iron and steel making facilities, including the three 175t converters, closed down in 2001.* *(All 10/86)*

1

"BR Blue, Class 37 Picture Gallery"

2

No.1 :	**37304** 6C24, Severn Tunnel Junction - Cardiff Tidal.	Empty 2-axle Steel carriers (mostly SEAs)
No.2 :	**37229 'Cardiff Rod Mill'** 8A86, East Usk - Margam	Coal (MDVs)
No.3 :	**37069 'Thornaby TMD'** 9Z03, Llanelli - Severn Tunnel Junction	Ballast (ZFV 'Dogfish' - 2 axle ballast wagons)
No.4 :	**37147** 9A96, Newport Docks - Severn Tunnel Junction	Departmental OBAs / MDVs

Newport, Alexandra Dock Junction

(top right) : *Class 60 No.60072 'Cairn Toul' is seen negotiating Ebbw Junction, Newport, after coming off the Down Cardiff Curve with 6B83, Ebbw Vale - Margam empty steel formed of a single IWA 'Cargowaggon'.*

Meanwhile, an unidentified EWS Class 66/0 and a pair of Class 37s (No.37412 + No.37419) await the signal to proceed.

(Opposite)

(top left) : *It's late afternoon and a busy time at Alexandra Dock Junction (ADJ) with plenty of activity.*

Class 60 No.60001 'The Railway Observer' heads down the Up Relief line with a rake of empty HAA, 2-axle, MGR coal hoppers, running as 6G45, Aberthaw - Avonmouth, which is normally a Class 66/0 turn.

In the yard, from left to right:

- No.60094 + 60097 on 6M17, Newport ADJ - Wembley 'Enterprise', formed mainly of chemical traffic containers from Barry Docks.

- An unidentified Class 66/0 will work forward with 6M17 to Warrington.

- Class 37s, No.37419 and No.37412 top 'n' tail 6B50, loaded ballast from Machen Quarry.

(bottom left) : *This is the same vantage point as that for No.60001, behind McDonalds fast food restaurant on the B4237. Here, EWS 'shed' No.66018 is in the process of propelling some steel carriers from ADJ yard to Newport Docks into Waterloo Loop, as this is the only way wagons can access the docks directly from ADJ yard.*

Trains arriving from the west can access the Docks branch directly, by leaving the Down Relief line at Alexandra Dock Junction, which No.66018 is about to pass.

(right) : *In glorious summer sunshine, Transrail Class 37/4 No.37412 'Loch Lomond' snakes across the points at Ebbw Junction with 6B50, ballast from Machen Quarry. No.37412 is at the other end of the train, out of view.*

The train will eventually reverse off the main line in to ADJ yard. Normally, ballast trains between Machen and ADJ run to East Usk, via the Gaer Single Line (Park Junction to Gaer Junction), reverse, and then run to ADJ.

As it was not possible for a loco to run round at Machen Quarry, operationally, 6B50 ran in top 'n' tail mode. *(All 06/01)*

Setting The Scene

Peak Forest in Microcosm

Apparently, a microcosm is a community, place, or situation regarded as encapsulating in miniature the characteristics of something much larger: in this instance, the railway system at Peak Forest is a microcosm of the modern rail network.

This was always an area I wanted to visit, particularly when Class 40s worked limestone trains in the area, but my work and other commitments prevented me from doing so. I had to wait until the early 2000s before time became available and, whilst the 40s had long gone, the area was rich in Class 60 activity - in fact, near 100% saturation, save for a twice-weekly 'out & back' Class 37 'Enterprise' trip running between Warrington Arpley and Dowlow.

"What's so special about Peak Forest", I hear you ask :

The main attraction is similar to that of Barnetby; a plethora of semaphore signalling, signal boxes and great photographic locations, not to mention Class 60 traction, which also pulled in a large number of photographers far and wide.

All freight traffic is limestone based, originating from the massive Dove Holes quarry or the limestone / cement works at Tunstead. All freight can be seen within a short distance, basically between the south portal of Dove Holes Tunnel through Peak Forest to Great Rocks. In fact, as many of the through freights to Tunstead usually pause at Peak Forest, it is possible to get two shots; one at Peak Forest and a second at Great Rocks.

The only disadvantage is that Peak Forest is not served by a direct passenger service, the nearest station being Buxton, so a car is essential.

Many enthusiasts are quite content busying themselves on or around two road bridges, which can be located on an Ordnance Survey Landranger Map (No.119 Buxton & Matlock) at:

Peak Forest	Grid reference	092 768
Great Rocks	Grid Reference	096 756

A Little History

There used to be a station at Peak Forest, which opened in 1867 by the Midland Railway on its extension of the Manchester, Buxton, Matlock & Midlands Junction Railway from Rowsley, forming part of the main Midland Line from Manchester to London. It closed in 1967 and the platforms demolished, although the station building survived as offices for the nearby quarry.

Locos are now stabled in Peak Forest Holding Sidings, south west of the old station, instead of running back & forth to Buxton depot, which is now closed. The depot was also used from 1994 to 1997 as a fuelling point until fuelling facilities were installed at Peak Forest.

Dove Holes Tunnel

To reach Peak Forest, the railway had to bore through the gritstone and limestone under Cow Low resulting in the construction of Dove Holes tunnel, 1 mile 1,224 yards long and some 183 feet beneath the current main passenger line to Buxton. It took five years to complete.

The southern entrance is at the summit of the line, nearly 1,000 feet above sea level, and descends nearly a hundred feet at a gradient of 1 in 90. The climb in the opposite direction is equally as gruelling, at 1 in 90,

As we have seen elsewhere, the Peak Forest route did not survive 'Beeching', nor this Trans-Pennine route, save for the section of line still in use today for freight traffic.

(opposite) : Two-tone grey Class 60, albeit now sporting EWS 'Beasties' sticker, No.60014 'Alexander Fleming' emerges from the south portal of Dove Holes tunnel with 6M17, Leeds Stourton - Peak Forest empty RMC bogie aggregate hoppers.

Apart from damp rails causing wheelslip, the tunnel became extremely hot in summer while, in winter, long icicles would form from the roof. By the time of diesel traction, there were a number of broken windscreens and for this reason, the Buxton snowplough was fitted with ice clearing equipment. (07/06)

EWS
014

(above) : *On the other side of the wall on Dale Road (which leads from the A6 to Peak Forest), No.60018 passes the last bit of its journey with* 6M17, Leeds Stourton - Peak Forest empties. (05/07)

(below) : *No.60075 is on its way to the holding sidings after earlier working in to Peak Forest. Meanwhile, No.60010 pauses alongside the old station building at Peak Forest with 6E52 to Peterborough, a trainload of stone loaded in MBA 'Monster' bogie box wagons.*

Note the BRA wagon, exactly the same in appearance to the BYA bogie steel carrier, but used as a coupling adapter to the Class 60. *(07/06)*

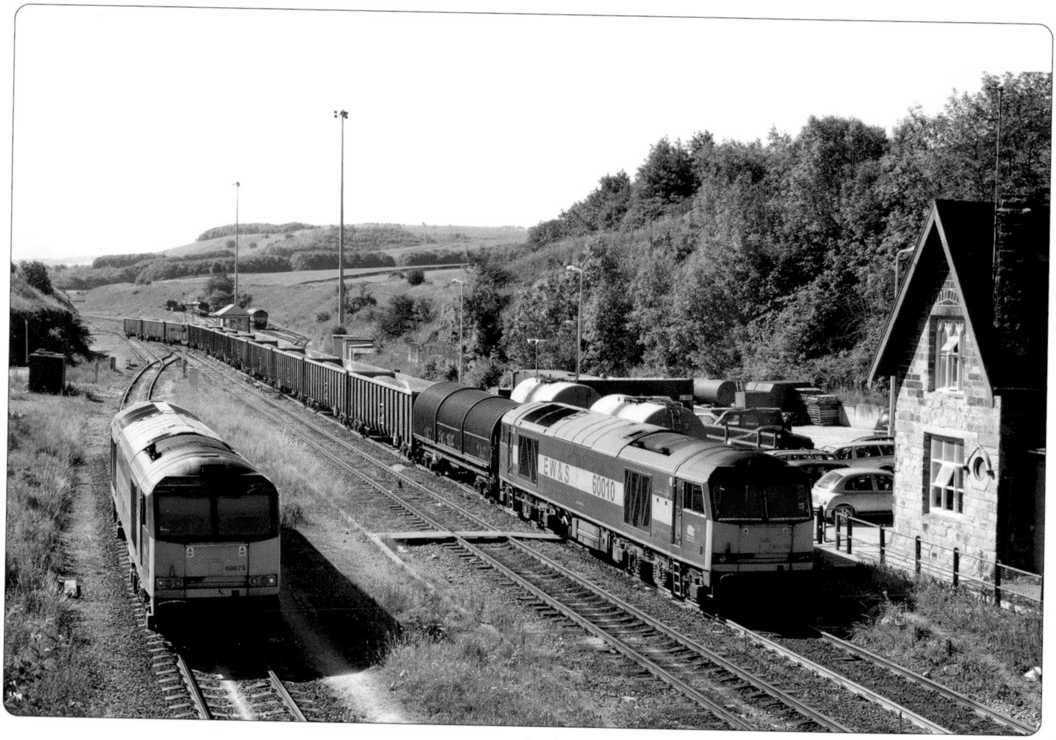

(above) : *'Classic' motive power and 'classic' wagons .... former Transrail Class 60 No.60082 arrives at Peak Forest with 6H55, ex-Bletchley. These distinctive wagons could be seen on flows of limestone emanating from Dove Holes quarry to receiving terminals at Manchester Hope Street, Leeds Stourton, Selby, Ely, Bletchley and Washwood Heath (Birmingham).* (05/07)

RMC JGA Bogie Aggregate Hoppers

These iconic hoppers were unique on flows emanating from Peak Forest until newer wagons came on stream, when the JGAs were dispersed for use on other stone flows around the network

Built between 1984 - 1997.

(right) : RMC 17235.

(below) : RMC 13709.

(bottom right) : RMC 19235.

(left) : *Two-tone grey and Mainline branded No.60086 'Schiehallion' is seen passing through Peak Forest with 6H03, Oakleigh - Tunstead empty Brunner Mond bogie limestone hoppers.*

These hoppers, built in 2000 by W H Davis (Shirebrook) are only used on this service. 07/05)

Brunner Mond (now Tata Chemicals Europe) is principally involved with the manufacture of products such as soda ash, sodium bicarbonate, calcium chloride and associated alkaline chemicals.

The original company was formed as a partnership in 1873 by John Brunner and Ludwig Mond. They built the Winnington Works in Northwich, and produced their first soda ash in 1874.

(below) : *Another view of No.60018 at Peak Forest, but this image is to illustrate the new EWS hoppers.*

These hoppers (Carkind HOA) were built in 2005 - 2006 by Wagony Swidnica, Poland, and numbered in the range 320000 - 320067.

Some of the first vehicles in the fleet were originally branded 'Cemex'.

PEAK FOREST

The nerve centre for operations in and around Peak Forest is the signal box, controlling the passage of freight services to the north and south of here. Peak Forest South signal box is located between the Up Main line (in front of the signal box) and the Holding Sidings.

The 'box is a Midland Railway Company type 4d design, opened by the London Midland & Scottish Railway Company (LMS) in July 1925 to replace a 1891-built signal box located on the opposite side of the line. In July 1974, the original lever frame was replaced by a 50 lever London Midland Region Standard frame.

(above) : *An unnamed No.60004 hauls a consist of loaded MEA, 2-axle, box wagons out of the Down & Up Through Siding, which forms 6H56, Dowlow - Ashbury.* (07/05)

Two images, taken from the hillside on the 'Up' side of the running lines, albeit at different elevations.

(above) : *The first depicts* No.60017 *'Shotton Works Centenary Year 1996' drawing into the Long Sidings with 6M11, Washwood Heath - Peak Forest and it will shortly propel the rake into the quarry to be loaded with another payload of limestone. Note the loco has white numbers and EWS branding in the gold band on the bodyside.*

(below) : *It's a busy day for No.60018 and it is now seen waiting to leave on the Up Goods Line with 6H96, Tunstead - Bredbury loaded stone. The consist is three HOA hoppers and quite a few former National Power hoppers, which are now used on this flow and one to Pendleton.*

When National Power were in the freight sector, they operated two types of wagon:

JMA	:	NP 19601 - 19682	Gascoigne Wood - Drax MGR coal circuit.
JHA	:	NP 19400 - 19420	Tunstead - Drax limestone.

(05/07)

GREAT ROCKS JUNCTION

From Great Rocks Junction the main line continues northwards to Peak Forest and Chinley as double track. The junction is controlled by Great Rocks Signal box, just below the overbridge here.

In the opposite direction, one line is the Down and Up Tunstead Siding, giving access to Tunstead Works and sidings.

The other, Down & Up Goods, line goes straight on as single track via Great Rocks tunnel and Topley Pike to Buxton.

The signal box at Great Rocks is a Midland Railway Company type 4d design fitted with a 34 lever Tappet frame, opened by the LMS in March 1923. It replaced an 1891-built signal box at the same site.

The signal box was rebuilt with a flat roof in the mid-1970s.

(top) : *No.60021 'Star of the East' takes the line to Tunstead Works with 6H03, Oakleigh - Tunstead empties, formed of unique JEA 'Brunner Mond' hoppers - see inset.* *(05/07)*

(right) : *No.60031 'ABP Connect' slows to take the line into Tunstead Works with 6M22, Leeds Hunslet - Tunstead cement empties, formed of JGA bogie cement tank hoppers.* *(07/06)*

The Hindlow 'Trip'

6H22, Tunstead - Hindlow

The 'Trip'

Limestone for the Lime plant at Hindlow is sourced from Tunstead and 'tripped' to Hindlow.

The 'trip' is particularly interesting because it is operationally complex and involves run-rounds, despite a journey distance of about 11 miles.

There are three legs:

1. Tunstead - Great Rocks Jct.
2. Great - Rocks Jct. - Buxton
3. Buxton - Hindlow

Timings

6H22, Tunstead - Hindlow

Mi. Ch	Location	Arr.	Dep.
0.00	**Tunstead Sdgs**		**10:20**
0.73	Great Rocks Jct *service runs round here*	10:27	10:47
2.21	Topley Pike Gf	*pass*	10:56
5.19	Buxton Signal Box *service exchanges token*	11:05	11:07
5.61	Buxton Up reception Siding *service loco runs around here*	11:09	11:29
6.23	Buxton Signal Box *service exchanges token*	11:31	11:33
11.11	**Briggs I.C.I. Sdgs**	**11:55**	

History

Hindlow Quarry was started by Briggs & Sons in 1882. In 1958, the practice of hand sorting and loading stone at the quarry face into narrow gauge rail wagons ended. Mechanisation took over with electric shovels and dump trucks transferring stone to a new crushing plant.

Between 1965 and 1988 three lime grinding mills were installed in the grinding plant. The site now has two highly automated Maerz PFR natural gas red kilns and three grinding mills that enable premium lime products to be produced using sustainable and environmentally positive methods.

A kiln is used for the calcination of limestone (calcium carbonate) to produce the form of lime called quicklime (calcium oxide). There are many uses for lime, including:

- in sugar production when purifying the juice from beet or cane
- natural calcium carbonate products used by farmers as animal feed.
- Quicklime, for basic oxygen steelmaking and production of aerated concrete blocks.
- Slaked Lime: used to make plaster, mortar, and limewash.

Limestone is brought from Tunstead to Hindlow, as illustrated on the opposite page. It's worth noting that Dowlow quarry is next to Hindlow, which despatches trainloads of limestone.

6H22

(1) (middle) : *After arriving at Tunstead light engine from Peak Forest, No.60021 'Star of the East' has collected its payload and waits for the road at Great Rocks with 6H22, loaded limestone hoppers (not in view) for Hindlow. (07/05)*

(2) (above) : *6H22 then runs to the bi-directional siding where the loco will run round. On this day, No.60053 'Nordic Chemical' is the train loco and, having completed the manoeuvre, prepares for the next leg to Buxton Sidings. (05/07)*

(3) (Page 98, overleaf) : *Now on the Buxton - Hindlow single line section, No.60018 ambles through the picturesque Derbyshire countryside heading for Hindlow.*

The line has some interesting features, such as Hindlow tunnel (514 yards long) and a summit, standing at 1,192ft above sea level. (05/07)

(right) : *The destination is now only a matter of yards away for No.60018 as it passes under the road bridge which gives access to the Works off the A515 at Sterndale Moor. The lorry in view is delivering Eden Water coolers. (05/07)*

EWS
60021

EWS
60500

Tunstead Works

(above) : *As I drove from Peak Forest to Great Rocks, I was afforded a great view of Tunstead Works.*

CHAPEL-en-le-FRITH

(previous page) : *A superb location .... making my way home, I stopped off near Chapel-en-le-Frith and positioned myself near the north portal of the 204 yard long Chapel LNW tunnel. Looking west, No.60500 'Rail Magazine' waits for a 'green' signal to proceed with 6M11, Washwood Heath - Peak Forest RMC empties. The loco was originally No.60016 'Langdale Pikes', renamed & renumbered to celebrate the 500th edition of 'Rail' magazine.*

(below) : *EWS 'Beasties' No.60014 'Alexander Fleming' is seen for a final time, heading away from the mouth of the tunnel with 6H96, Tunstead - Bredbury loaded limestone.* *(07/06)*

"The Shape of things to Come"

When I visited Peak Forest, the ubiquitous General Motors Class 66s were becoming a more common sight; EWS Class 66/0s, plus Freightliner Heavy Haul 66/6s and their own fleet of purpose built HIA limestone hoppers, were taking over.

In fact, fast forward 10 years to 2017, there would not be a single working allocated Class 60 traction!

(above) : *FHH Class 66/6 No.66606 passes through Peak Forest with 6M03, Barrow Hill - Tunstead.*

(below) : *EWS Class 66/0 No.66080 waits to leave the Tunstead Works at Great Rocks Junction with 7H96, Tunstead - Bredbury loaded limestone.* (07/05)

Setting The Scene

Apart from a few exceptions - the Settle & Carlisle readily springs to mind - I prefer taking photographs at places with plenty of interest, with provenance to identify location, especially industrial landscapes and Teesside fits the bill perfectly.

Why Teesside, and here I mean south of the River Tees. There is a plethora of interesting locations and interest, not to mention plenty of Class 56 and Class 60 activity. Teesside industry is dominated primarily by steelmaking (eg. British Steel), chemical manufacture (eg. Imperial Chemical Industries (ICI)) and imported coal through Redcar.

In its heyday, Teesside Steelworks was a large expanse of steelworks that formed a continuous stretch along the south bank of the River Tees from Middlesbrough to Redcar. At its height there were 91 blast furnaces within a 10 mile radius but, by the late 1970s, there was only one left on Teesside. Opened in 1979, located near the mouth of the River Tees, the Redcar blast furnace was the second largest in Europe. The majority of the steelworks, including the Redcar blast furnace, Redcar and South Bank coke oven and the BOS plant at Lackenby closed in 2015. The Teesside Beam Mill and some support services still operate at Lackenby.

Latterly, growth in freight traffic has developed through Teesport, the third largest port in the United Kingdom, mainly associated with the local petrochemical, chemical and steel processing industries.

Locations

I must confess, as much as I liked the area, I did not fully explore all the possible photographic locations, concentrating as such on those illustrated in the next few pages:

- Eaglescliffe
- Thornaby
- Tees Yard
- Middlesbrough
- Grangetown

Thornaby

Thornaby TMD was a railway Traction Maintenance Depot, operated by DB Schenker, situated to the east of Thornaby, on the northern side of the line to Middlesbrough.

BR began construction in 1957, building its last roundhouse for steam locos, developed on a 70 acre site for the shed and its associated facilities alone, it comprised:

- a 300ft diameter octagonal roundhouse, containing 22 sidings accessed via a 70ft turntable.
- running shed with covered preparation sheds and wet ash pits
- A repair shed with wheeldrops, blacksmith, coppersmith and machine shop
- A 350 tonnes mechanised coaling plant, capable of fuelling four locos simultaneously

The shed opened in June 1958, allocated a code of 51L and took over the allocation of locos at Newport (51B), Middlesbrough (51D) plus, a year later, Stockton (51E) and Haverton Hill (51G), all of which eventually closed.

At this time the depot had the largest allocation of any single depot in the country, although Stratford (30A) had a larger allocation but were shared with 6 sub-sheds. The depot was closed to steam in December 1964.

In the diesel era, under TOPS, the depot code was changed to 'TE' and the depot adopted a White Kingfisher logo which was applied to the sides of their locos.

Early allocations included Class 03, 04, 08, 17, 25, 27 and 37s. In later years, 25s and 27s had been replaced by Class 20, 31, 47 and 56s. The depot closed in 2009 and the buildings demolished two years later.

Tees Yard

As part of the 1950s British Railways modernisation plan, a project evolved to centralise the marshalling of goods wagons and the associated servicing of steam locos at the UK's largest freight hub. There were a number of marshalling yards servicing coal mines and steel mills at Consett, West County Durham and North Yorkshire, as well as those for Middlesbrough Dock. The decision was taken to rationalise these to one yard, Tees Marshalling Yard.

The yard was initially developed as a hump shunting facility but, by the time construction had been completed in 1963, wagon-shunting ceased, replaced by containerisation and Merry-go-round (MGR) trains.

Furthermore, with rationalisation in both coal mining and steel making, the yard closed in stages from 1985 with the run-down of rail freight in the area. Following the closure of Middlesbrough Dock in 1980 and the development of Teesport, Thornaby became isolated from its main source of traffic.

The Down Yard is completely closed apart from the Down Staging sidings which remain open to all freight operators. The Up yard remains busy shunting traffic for the nearby steel works and as a staging point for long distance flows. The Yard now consists of Arrivals and Departures at the Thornaby end:

- 1 to 5 for Departures.
- 6 to 12 for Arrivals.

There is also a shunt neck leading to 42 Primary sorting sidings.

Thornaby East Junction (opposite) : *This is a view of Thornaby East Junction, as seen from the north side of the track, looking back towards the west end of the depot. The lines you can see, from left to right, are:*

nearside	middle	Far right
Line 1 : Down Goods	Line 3 : Down Arrival / Up Departure	Up' Goods No.1
Line 2 : Up Goods No.2	Line 4 : Loco Line	Down main line
	Others : Washer'	Up main line
	Loco Depot (arr/dep)	

A Class 185 Trans-pennine Express DMU, No.185 119, passes on the Up Main with a service from Middlesbrough to Manchester Airport.

Eaglescliffe

Just north of Eaglescliffe station, at Witham Hall, I found a footbridge over the line, a great vantage point from where to photograph freight traffic, especially southbound services.

The line is only about a mile south of Stockton Cut Junction, so I could see freight here from three different sources:

- Tees Yard and further east.
- Durham Coast line via Hartlepool and Sunderland.
- Stillington 'freight-only' branch to Ferryhill.

On a subsequent visit to this location 10 years later, access to the footbridge had been closed off. This left only the station itself at Eaglescliffe, which was not quite the same.

(above) : *Transrail Class 56 No.56127 heads along the Up main line at Eaglescliffe with a fully laden 4L79, the 16:13 Wilton - Felixstowe freightliner, a time when Thornaby based 56s worked the Felixstowe 'liners.* *(04/97)*

(below) : *Without the provision of 'Gen' (ie. TOPS reports) it was impossible to identify MGR coal workings which, for the most part, worked to STP (Short Term Trainplan) schedules based on a power station's demand for coal. Here, Loadhaul 'grid' No.56006 'Ferrybridge C power station' passes through Eaglescliffe station with an unidentified rake of empty MGR, 2-axle, HAA hoppers.*

The train would have arrived here from the south after taking the 'freight only' line from Northallerton and Yarm, but not the Darlington route which the 'Pacer' waiting at the station will take, leading off to the right. *(04/97)*

THORNABY

The station lies on the original Stockton & Darlington Railway extension to Middlesbrough and it's docks at Port Darlington, as they were known. The station is now just a simple island platform, used by rail enthusiasts wishing to visit Tees Yard. The lines from Middlesbrough converge here along with those serving Tees Yard, while the Down Goods line runs from Thornaby East Junction for nearly two miles on the north side of Tees Yard before joining up with the Middlesbrough main line at Newport East Junction.

(above) : *It should have been a 'tug', but no matter, a little variation. EWS Class 66/0 No.66129 comes off the Down Main on to the Down Goods at Thornaby with 6N85, Aldwarke - Tees Dock steel wire, loaded on SPA, 2-axle, steel carriers. The train could also convey steel rods.*

(below) : *Slowly pulling away from Tees Yard, No.60018 is about to pass the station with 6M46, Redcar - Hardendale empty limestone hoppers, which is formed of two portions; CBA 'Covhops' (nearest the camera) from Lackenby and HGAs from Redcar.*

Thornaby MPD

(above) : *This is the eastern end of Thornaby depot where many locos can be seen, some outside the shed and others in the sidings nearest the camera, housing mainly withdrawn or stored locos and wagons.*

The two 56s looking in reasonable condition are EWS-liveried No.56103 'Sister Dora' and Loadhaul No.56109.

This vantage point is an overbridge which spans both the depot and Tees Yard on Teesside Park Drive, which can be accessed off the B6541, Middlesbrough Road.

Thornaby 'Tractors'

No.37506 (middle)

Transferred to Thornaby : January 1987

Named 'British Steel Skinningrove'.

Livery : BR Railfreight Grey, Large Logo.

No.37511 (left)

Transferred to Thornaby : January 1987

Named 'Stockton Haulage'.

Livery : Two tone Grey,
Freight Metals decals

(09/88)

Thornaby 'Down Main'

(above) : *I was busy photographing some 56s in Tees Yard from the overbridge which spans the yard, without realising straightaway that a Class 56-hauled freight was fast approaching on the 'Down' main line.*

I quickly ran along the road to position myself and just about made it in time, although I would have preferred a better composition. However, I am glad I at least got a shot, as this is the only time I have seen, let alone photograph, a pipe train. Here is No.56094 'Eggborough Power Station' just about to pass under the road bridge with 6E67, the 07:08 Stanton Gate - Tees Dock loaded train of mostly 'large' pipes for export.

The pipes are being conveyed on bogie bolster wagons with a small, open, wagon sandwiched in between each bolster wagon to manage any overhang of the large pipes.

Tees Yard

(above) : *One of the attractions of Teesside was that the majority of freight traffic was in the hands of Class 56s. In this view, I had two 'Grids' in shot.*

EWS Class 56 No.56087 has arrived in the yard with 6N15, Hartlepool - Tees Yard empty steel coil carriers, which will return to South Wales later the same day. Meanwhile Transrail liveried No.56099 slowly passes through with MEAs loaded with coal, running as 6Z84, Redcar - Ketton cement works.

(left) : *On the far left, No.56071 waits on the Up Goods No.2 line with 6F78, Middlesbrough Goods - Boulby empty rock salt 'Covhops' and will enter the yard via Transfer Line 2 (see opposite).*

Meanwhile, Class 60 No.60001 'The Railway Observer' pulls out of the Up yard with 6M46, Redcar - Hardendale limestone empties. The train is a combination of CBA 'Covhops' from Lackenby and HGA hoppers from Redcar, located at the front and rear of the train, resepctively.

(right) : *Exhaust fumes gently waft away from No.56081 as it ticks over, ready to leave with Sunday's 6N52, Tees Yard - Tees Dock 'Enterprise', formed of empty containerised chemicals, which arrived the previous day from Carlisle.*

This traffic was simply known as the 'Hoyer' train, which was a daily train of containerised chemicals from Tees Dock to Carlisle Yard (6M57), going forward to Workington.

The first two wagons in this consist are FKA, EWS intermodal low platform flats.

(below) : *Class 56 No.56071 now waits on the transfer line with 6F78 empty rock salt hoppers. The train has to run to Tees Yard to reverse, as there is no direct access in or out of Middlesbrough Goods to the east for Boulby traffic.*

In the foreground, Class 60 No.60042 'The Hundred of Hoo', has just arrived with 6F46, Skinningrove - Tees Yard loaded steel. Skinningrove (on the Boulby branch) produces high quality steel products, especially for marine industrial use.

A19 Tees Viaduct

The A19 Tees Viaduct or Tees Flyover is a high level, six-lane, dual carriageway, which I used as a vantage point to photograph passing freight traffic. I reached the road level by climbing a stairway by the side of one of the columns on the south side of the main line. As it was a Sunday, there was little traffic, although I was worried about passing police cars whilst I was on the top.

Fortunately, I was able to take some photographs unhindered and they certainly are breathtaking views of Tees Yard to the west and Newport Bridge to the east.

The Viaduct is west of Middlesbrough, close to the A19 interchange, and crosses the River Tees, the goods lines out of the yard, the main line and the B6541 road. The bridge was built between 1973 and 1975 and is 1.8 miles long, 1.2 miles between abutments - the largest span is over the river, at 128ft.

rRight) : *The 'Hoyer' train.*

Class 56 No.56081 is seen again, this time from the top of the A19 Flyover, heading along the Up Goods No.1 line with 6M57, Tees Dock - Carlisle Yard containerised chemicals 'Enterprise' service.

In the background (far right) is the iconic Tees Transporter Bridge in Middlesbrough. This image gives a good indication of its scale, the beam is 160ft above the ground.

(opposite) : *Looking west. Having already arrived with 6N61, Tyne Yard - Lackenby (ex-Hardendale), and dropped off the Redcar portion, No.60028 'John Flamsteed' now heads east paset the Engineer's Sidings en-route to Lackenby.*

John flamsteed (1646 - 1719) was the first Astronomer Royal.

(below) : *From the same vantage point, but this time with a splendid backdrop of the Newport Bridge, two-tone grey Class 60 No.60092 'Reginald Munns' heads west with a long rake of empty steel carriers - 'BEAs' / 'BNAs' - running as 6D11, Lackenby - Scunthorpe.*

A Little History

Newport Bridge

This is a vertical-lift bridge spanning the River Tees, built by Dorman Long and was the first large vertical-lift bridge in Britain, a short distance to the west of the Tees Transporter Bridge, linking Middlesbrough with Stockton-on-Tees. It was completed in 1934 and no longer lifts, but still acts as a road bridge in a permanently down position.

The bridge was inaugurated by the future King George VI and opened to traffic in February 1934. Its vital statistics read: twin 180ft lifting towers, 269ft bridge span, weighing 2,700 tonnes, with the bridge capable of being raised to 121ft.

Tees (Middlesbrough) Transporter Bridge

The opening ceremony in October 1911 was performed by the 'Prince Arthur of Connaught', painted red for some reason, and connects Middlesbrough to Port Clarence. It is a transporter bridge, carrying a travelling 'gondola', suspended from the bridge, which can carry 200 people and 9 cars. It now links Middlesbrough and Port Clarence.

The overall length (including cantilevers) is 851ft, leaving a span between the towers of 590 feet, the beam of the bridge being carried at a height of 160ft above the road. It has the distinction of being the the longest remaining transporter bridge in the world.

Cargo Fleet

The two images on these two pages were taken from a road bridge which leads from a roundabout on the A66 and then crosses the main line to the B1513 on the other side. I parked my car just off road and was afforded great views in both directions, although the view is completely different today.

(left) : *The industrial backdrop of South Bank and Grangetown is the setting for Mainline Class 37 No.37372, which is seen sweeping round the curve at Cargo Fleet with a shortish rake of loaded steel slabs, running as a 'special' on this particular occasion, possibly heading for Etruria, Stoke on Trent.*

The concrete tower on the left is part of the coking plant at South Bank (now demolished) and, on the right, Lackenby steelworks at Grangetown, which has survived to the present day. (04/97)

(opposite) : *Looking in the opposite direction, there is plenty of interest to attract your attention.*

Loadhaul Class 56 No.56090 heads east with empty rock salt wagons, which is 6P83, the 09:06 Middlesbrough Goods - Boulby. The train needed to head to Tees Yard first, in order to reverse and proceed east.

On the right is the Riverside Stadium, the new home of Middlesbrough Football Club, following their move from Ayresome park.

On the left is the small, now closed, Cargo Fleet station halt, and the signal box, only acting as a gate box for a crossing at the time of my visit. (04/97)

35
W
27
090

Teesside Freight Wagons

Boulby Traffic

Potash / Rock Salt

(left) : **JGA Bogie Covered Hopper**
Original NACCO Salt JGAs
Built 1998 by Arbel Fauvet, France.
Nos. 70. 0894. 100 - 152
Image NACO 19260 at Grangetown.

(middle): **JIA Bogie Covered Hopper**
Built 1997 by Arbel Fauvet, France.
Nos. 70. 0894. 100 - 152
Image 70. 0894. 130 at Grangetown.

(below) : **JGA Bogie Covered Hopper**
Former Cleveland Potash JGAs.
Built 1991 by W. H. Davis
Nos. NACO 17450 - 17456
Image NACO 17453 at Grangetown.

(above) : **Redcar traffic**
HGA 2-axle Lime Hopper
Built 1975 by Standard Wagon
Nos. 362000 - 362111
Image *No.362015 - Tees Yard*

Limestone

(below) : **Lackenby traffic**
CBA 2-Axle Covered Limestone Hopper
Built 1975 by BREL, Ashford
Nos. 362150 - 362199
Image *No.362162 - Thornaby*

Grangetown Junction

Where?

This is where the line to Tees Dock (Teesport) leaves the main line to Redcar and Saltburn.

I take the A1053, off the A66, at a roundabout in the shadow of Lackenby steelworks, the road gently climbing to another roundabout, which leads to Tees Dock. This provides an excellent vantage point form where I was able to view passing freight traffic, plus that which accessed the Port.

Beforehand, as the road passes under a railway line leading from Lackenby to Tees Dock, there is a lay-by, opposite Grangetown Junction signal box where I could park my car. From there, walking up to the roundabout, I could take photographs from the road or nearby England Coast Path.

One added bonus, I could observe the Boulby - Tees Dock Potash trains at close quarters and, as these trains had to reverse in the goods loop by the signal box to gain access to & from the Port, it was a fantastic location.

Traffic

By far the majority of traffic to be seen here is Potash and Rock Salt, originating from the Boulby Mine to Tees Dock and Middlesbrough Goods, respectively. The mine is located south of Loftus along the route of the former Whitby, Redcar & Middlesbrough Union Railway, which was closed in May 1958, but remained open between Saltburn and Boulby for freight traffic. Sample flows are shown opposite.

Potash was first discovered in 1939, in and around Aislaby when prospectors were drilling, hoping to find oil. The reserves were investigated in the 1950s but appeared too deep to exploit economically and it was not until 1968 when the first shaft was sunk; Imperial Chemical Industries (ICL) started to construct the mine a year later, but full production did not commence until 1976. The mine became the source of all of the UK's home-produced potash.

What is potash & rock salt?

Potash is an 'umbrella' term that covers all the bases of potassium-bearing minerals, found in large evaporated deposits from ancient lakes, sea beds or rock formations. The mined ore sourced at Boulby consists of 35–45% potash (potassium chloride) and 45–55% halite (rock salt, or sodium chloride).

Potash is generally used as fertiliser, but also added as food seasoning and in brewing beer. The rock salt is extracted as a by-product and used across the UK as a de-icing agent on roads.

Boulby Traffic

Potash

Location	***arr.***	***dep.***	
Boulby Mine Carlin How		**09:33**	
Crag Hall S.B.	09:49	09:50	Exchange Token
Saltburn West Jct.	pass	10:14	
Marske	pass	10:16	
Longbeck	pass	10:17	
Redcar East	pass	10:18	
Redcar Central	pass	10:20	
British Steel Redcar	pass	10:23	
Redcar Ore Terminal Jct.	pass	10:24	
Shell Junction	pass	10:24	
Grangetown Junction	pass	10:25	
Grangetown (Cleveland)	10:26	10:46	Loco Runs Round
South Bank Tees Dock	**11:00**		

Rock Salt

Location	***arr.***	***dep.***	
Boulby Mine Carlin How		**09:33**	
Crag Hall S.B.	09:49	09:50	Exchange Token
Saltburn West Jct.	pass	10:14	
Marske	pass	10:16	
Longbeck	pass	10:17	
Redcar East	pass	10:18	
Redcar Central	pass	10:20	
British Steel Redcar	pass	10:23	
Redcar Ore Terminal Jct.	pass	10:24	
Shell Junction	pass	10:25	
Grangetown Junction	pass	10:26	
Grangetown (Cleveland)	pass	10:26½	
Beam Mill Jct.	pass	10:27	
South Bank	pass	10:28	
South Bank Jct.	pass	10:28½	
Whitehouse Jct.	pass	10;31	
Guisborough Jct	pass	10:34	
Middlesbrough	**pass**	**10:36**	
Newport East Jct	pass	10:38	
Tees Yard	10:43	11:03	Loco Runs Round
Newport East Jct	pass	11:07	
Middlesbrough Goods		**11:17**	

(opposite) : *Having arrived in the Down Goods Loop'besides Grangetown signal box, No.56115 'Barry Needham' is in the process of running round in order to take 6F62 (ex-Boulby) in to Tees Dock.*

Lackenby (above) : *Looking south from the roundabout at the entrance to Teesport, the view is an expanse of steel mills and sidings, part of the Lackenby steelworks complex. Class 56 No.56069 'Wolverhampton Steel Mill' is almost dwarfed in the shadow of its surroundings, as it makes its way to collect it's payload.*

Grangetown (above) : *Looking across the running lines, No.56032 sits in the Goods Loop with 6F61, Boulby - Tees Dock empty potash hoppers.*

"Snakes & Ladders"

(above) : *No.56032 is now on another trip to Boulby, this time working 6F76, potash empty 'Covhops' ex-Tees Dock, which is seen in the process of snaking over from the Down Goods onto the main line. The train will proceed to Saltburn West Junction, where it will diverge on to the Boulby branch, the mine being reached some 12 miles further down the branch, three-quarters of an hour later.*

(above) : **4E54** : *The distinctive bright orange containers with yellow 'UBC Bulk' branding, clearly identifies this working as 4E54, the 03:31 Trafford Park - Tees Dock intermodal. UBC (United Bulk Carriers) serve Tees Dock and have their own fleet of B, C, S and T-Class bulk carriers, conveying mostly chemical products.*

(below) : ***6N34, Redcar - Wilton*** : *This is, and still is, the shortest MGR coal working on the rail network which, as the crow flies, is no distance at all. However, 6N34 has to first run to Grangetown, reverse, and then retrace its route as far as Shell Junction, where Class 66/0 No.66042 will leave the former Stockton & Darlington / Middlesbrough & Redcar Railway and take the 'Wilton Branch' to I.C.I. Wilton.*

Freightliner

IBC
Freightliner
CLEVELAND POTASH

"FHH Takeover"

With effect, April 2007, Freightliner Heavy Haul (FHH) replaced EWS for the operational control and supply of motive power for all the Boulby traffic to Tees Dock and Middlesbrough Goods. At the same time, the reporting headcodes were also changed to become sequential - for example, 6F23, 6F24, 6F25 and 6F26, irrespective of running loaded or empty.

I paid a visit in August 2007 to photograph some of these new workings.

Potash Movements at Grangetown

6F32, 09:34 Boulby - Tees Dock

(top left) : *Class 66/5 No.66531 crosses from the Up main line to the Down Goods with loaded potash hoppers from Boulby. It will pull up alongside Grangetown signal box, reverse, and then go into the docks.*

(opposite, middle) : *The loco has been uncoupled, run round, and is now awaiting the signal to proceed down the docks branch with 6F32.*

6F23, the 09:48 Tees Dock - Boulby

(bottom, left) : *FHH Class 66/6 No.66607 cautiously makes its way out of the docks with 6F23 towards Grangetown Junction; the giant dockside cranes wait expectantly for the next shipment of containers.*

(above) : *I particularly like the industrial setting, which features the Dorman Long coking plant in South Bank, Middlesbrough, on the horizon, built between 1952 to 1957. This was a local landmark, clearly visible from the A66, as I drove towards Grangetown. FHH Class 66/6 No.66607 'snakes' its way from Grangetown and onto the main line with 6F23 bound for Boulby. This image became the front cover for Freightmaster No.49.*

Coatham Marsh
EWS
56071

Favourite Images

(above) : ***Class 60*** *No.60077 'Canisp' passes Grangetown Junction on the Down main line with 6N25, Tees yard - Redcar limestone, formed of HGA 2-axle lime hoppers. The train is passing Milepost 19, which is the mileage from Darlington.*

(left) : *Looking west from a railway overbridge at Coatham, a western suburb of Redcar,* ***Class 56*** *No.56071 makes a splendid composition at is passes Coatham Marshes nature reserve with 6F75, Tees Dock - Boulby potash empties.*

Westbury

Setting The Scene

Westbury is an important junction on the railway network, as it lies at the point where the following lines meet:

- London Paddington - Reading - Taunton
- Swindon
- Bath and Bristol
- Salisbury

The railway station is northwest of the town centre and a smaller station, Dilton Marsh, is to the southwest of the town centre, but this former 'halt' is now a request stop for passenger services.

Historical perspective

The station was opened by the Wilts, Somerset & Weymouth Railway (WS&WR) in September 1848 and was the initial terminus of the WS&WR line from Chippenham, which was later extended to Frome, opening in October 1850. The line to Salisbury opened in June 1856 and when the line opened between Patney and Chirton (1900), plus that further west from Castle Cary to Cogload Junction in 1906, the GWR new main line from London Paddington to Taunton was complete.

In 1899, Westbury station was entirely rebuilt, creating two island platforms which were six hundred feet long and forty feet wide. Of particular note, was the construction of the Westbury 'avoiding line', constructed in 1933 to remove delays caused by the 30mph passage through the station. By 1978, semaphore signalling had been replaced by MAS colour lights and a new signalling centre was built on a site to the east of the station.

In 2019, the platforms at the west end were lengthened to accommodate the new Great Western Railway IEP trains.

Freight Perspective

In many respects, rail freight is the main reason for Westbury's importance, dominated by huge tonnages of aggregate emanating from the Mendip quarries at Merehead and Whatley. As well as 'direct' trains to receiving terminals, there are also the so called 'jumbo' trains of 3,000 tonnes plus, which convey stone as far as Acton Yard, where these trains are split into two or three portions. These smaller trains then go forward to receiving terminals in and around London and the South East of England.

Westbury is important for these reasons:

- Traffic Centre for train crews and locos.
- extensive sidings to stage and store wagons.
- Virtual Quarry (VQ) to stockpile ballast.
- the formation of engineer's trains.

Getting There

Living in Swindon, Westbury was in easy reach for me, driving myself or taking the train, either way it was about one hour's journey time. Travelling by train was preferable, when using a direct service via Melksham (once on a 'freight-only' line) or via a change of trains at Bath Spa. Many enthusiasts content themselves at the station, where there are facilities for refreshments, etc.

Station Road bridge, immediately east of the station, affords good views in both directions, while a good 10-minutes furthe on, Hawkerbridge Road bridge provided a vantage point for trains:

- taking the Trowbridge line.
- avoiding Westbury on the Hawkerbridge Jct. - Westbury East Loop Jct., especially diversions.

Further afield, Fairwood Junction to the west of Westbury was my favourite location, but I needed my car to get there. Great views of all traffic, all day, including those using the station avoiding line.

WESTBURY STATION

(above) : *The station lies on a south west / north east orientation and is formed by two island platforms, although the far left platform is not in use and the line serves as the Down Reception for freight traffic. This panoramic view shows the layout and the yards beyond, as Class 59/2 No.59201 makes its way from the stabling point.* (05/09)

'Up Trowbridge'

(below) : *With a gleaming set of new IOA 'Gondola' empty ballast box wagons in tow, FHH Class 66/6 No.66602 heads away from Westbury on the Up Trowbridge line with 6U72, the 11:56 Westbury VQ - Stud Farm. The train will leave this line at Bradford Junction to take the single line to Thingley Junction. The loaded train from Stud Farm (6U73) arrives at Westbury at four o'clock in the morning.* (05/09)

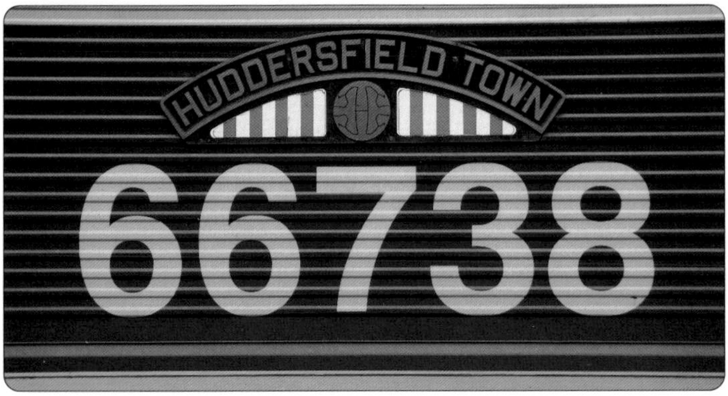

(above) : *DB Schenker Class 59/2 No.59203 has pulled in to the holding siding next to the Down eception’ line with 7O40, the 13:35 Merehead - Eastleigh loaded stone hoppers.*

The loco will uncouple, run round, and then proceed to take the line to Salisbury, which curves round to the left behind the rear JYA hopper. *(07/17)*

(middle) : *This train has been operated by EWS, FHH, GBRf and, at the time of writing, Colas Rail.*

GBRf Class 66/7 No.66738 ‘Huddersfield Town’ leaves the Up sidings with 6M40, the 11:56 Westbury VQ - Stud Farm empty IOA ‘Gondola’ ballast hoppers.

(left) : *The loco carries the name ‘Huddersfield Town’, one of six Class 66/7s locos named after famous football clubs, designed to be identical to those once carried by former LNER B17 4-6-0 steam locos.* *(09/17)*

(above) : *Hanson-liveried Class 59/1 No.59102 'Village of Chantry' waits at Westbury station for a driver to take forward 6L21, the 13:30 Whatley - Dagenham loaded stone. Colas Class 70 No.70801 is stabled in the yard along with a Class 153 Super Sprinter, which had worked in a service from Bristol Parkway. (06/16)*

(below) : *Colas Rail became a major player at Westbury from January 2014, taking over many workings from other operators including departmental services and engineer's trains to and from Bescot and Eastleigh. A busy scene greeted me on this visit with four Colas Class 70s on view, two of which are Nos.70806 and 70814, plus Super Sprinter No.153 708 stabled between the two rows of 70s. (08/2017)*

(above) : *Apart from HSTs (High Speed Train) and IEPs (Intercity Express Programme) working between London Paddington and the West of England, domestic services to Bristol, Swindon, Salisbury and Weymouth are in the hands of Class 153 and Class 158 DMUs. Super Sprinter No.153 370 departs Westbury with a local 'all stations' service to Worcester Shrub Hill.* (09/09)

(below) : *Following the collapse of the coal sector, many coal hoppers were re-deployed for use on aggregate trains. Some former HTA bogie coal hoopers (ie. the red ones!) are in the consist of 7B12, the 11:35 Merehead - Wootton Bassett loaded stone. No.59201 is the train engine, awaiting a driver.* (06/16)

(above) : *Sometimes a DBC (Deutsche Bahn Cargo) Class 60 finds itself at Westbury and is used as a 'super shunter', in place of a Class 08. While FHH Class 66/5 No.66588 waits in the 'Up reception' line with 6C72 from Fairwater Yard, Taunton, No.60039 'Dove Holes' is busy shunting wagons in the yard. Note also the new colour light signalling and the extended platform to accommodate the new IEP trains.* *(iPhone 7+ 09/19)*

(below) : *During GBRf's reign of working 6M40, Westbury VQ - Stud Farm ballast empties, Class 66/7 No.66731 'interhubGB' waits for No.153 305 to leave with 2M10, the 12:16 hrs service to Swindon. Train 6M40 will follow behind the unit all the way to Swindon, via Trowbridge and Melksham.* *(03/15)*

Wales & Wessex Trains

During the 1990s, there were more diesel hauled passenger services on the main line, such as those run by Wales & Wessex between Bristol Temple Meads and Weymouth. This diagram operated between 1th July - 13th September 1998:

2C64,	07:14	Westbury - Bristol Temple Meads	
2O86,	08:30	Bristol Temple Meads - Weymouth	
2V74,	11:03	Weymouth- Bristol Temple Meads	
2O90,	14:33	Bristol Temple Meads - Weymouth	
2V89,	17:20	Weymouth - Bristol Temple Meads	
5V89,	20:05	Bristol Temple Meads - Westbury	ECS

(above) : *Having made the Westbury station stop, EWS liveried Class 37/4 No.37411 'Ty Hafan' accelerates along the Down Trowbridge line at Heywood with 2V89, the 17:20 Weymouth - Bristol Temple Meads, formed of four Mk2a coaches - two in maroon livery, the other two in blue. One regret I do have is that I never travelled on one of these trains between Bristol and Weymouth - too busy photographing, such a shame!* (05/98)

The 'Warminster Incline'

The line to Salisbury leaves the Great Western line at Westbury South Junction. From level ground, the line climbs at a gradient of 1 in 75 until Dilton Marsh, followed by couple of miles at around 1 in 70 before levelling out again at Warminster. Warminster being the highest point on the line.

(above) : *The black horse in the field below the railway embankment seems completely uninterested in the thrash of the Class 59/2 as it accelerates up the incline with a heavy trainload of stone. This is 7O40, the 13:40 Merehead - Eastleigh, hauled by cherry red Class 59/2 No.59206, which is passing Penleigh on the western outskirts of Westbury on the way to Dilton Marsh halt.* *(09/09)*

(below) : *EWS 'sheds' No.66068 + No.66176 are double-heading 6O41, the 10:14 Westbury Yard - Eastleigh Yard departmental service on the 'Warminster Incline', viewed from Fairwood Road bridge, the point at which the road passes over the Westbury Avoiding Line. Unfortunately, the consist could not be seen.* *(02/10)*

Hawkeridge Junction

This is where the line from Trowbridge divides; straight on for another 50 chains to Westbury station, while a spur leads off to Westbury East Loop Junction. The double track curve is 35 chains long and is known as the 'East Loops', used by freight traffic going to and from the 'Berks & Hants' main line, plus as a diversionary route.

(above) : *This is one of the 'booked' freight services to use the 'East Loop', which is 6A21, the 08:28 Cardiff Pengam - Theale loaded stone. On this occasion the train engine is FHH Class 66/6 No.66611 and the consist is Bardon Aggregates JGA bogie hoppers.* (02/10)

Diverts (top left) : *Due to weekend engineering blockades between Didcot and Reading, some freightliners to Southampton were diverted via Swindon, Melksham, Westbury and Salisbury. Class 66/5 No.66503 slowly approaches Hawkeridge Junction with 4O54, the 05:33 Leeds - Southampton freightliner.* (04/05)

(bottom left) : *Meanwhile, No.66537 passes over the junction with 4O27, the 00:09 Ditton - Southampton.*

(below) : *Apart from the usual diet of aggregate, there was one notable service and this was 6V62, the 08:48 (TO) Fawley - Bristol / Plymouth fuel oil tanks. EWS Class 66/0 No.66039 passes Hawkeridge Junction with 6V62, formed of TTA 2-axle tank wagons, which are in the ESSO 56001 - 56279 number range.* (07/09)

Fairwood

Fairwood Road links Dilton Marsh and Fairwood, crossing both the Westbury Avoiding Line and the main line serving Westbury station, the road bridge at the latter point is featured here. There are good views, especially for westbound shots, where Westbury White Horse can also be included.

(above) : *Hanson-liveried Class 59/1 No.59102 "Village of Chantry' approaches with 7C77, the 12:40 Acton Yard - Merehead empty 'Jumbo' stone train, formed of perhaps 2/3 'portions'* *(05/09)*

(opposite) : *This shot is actually taken from the overbridge at Fairwood Junction. Class 59/0 No.59005 'Kenneth J Painter' sweeps round the curve with 6C74, the 13:15 Theale - Whatley empty 'Hanson' JGA stone hoppers. 6C74, plus some of the 'Jumbo' stone trains are booked to go via the avoiding line.* *(06/09)*

(below) : *"Two for the Price of One" .... 7A17, the 10:31 Merehead - Acton Yard formed of two portions of loaded stone in IIA bogie hoppers and JNA box wagons. Traction is in the shape of EWS Class 59/2 No.59205 and Aggregates Industries-liveried Class 59/0 No.59001 'Yeoman Endeavour'.* *(05/09)*

"A Tale of Two Liveries"

(above) : *The Class 59/1 locos were built in 1990 by General Motors, London, Ontario, Canada, and there are four locos in the fleet - Nos.59101 - 59104 - all named after villages in the Mendips, close to the operational base at Whatley Quarry, owned by Hanson who also own the locos. This broadside view shows off the Hanson colours of dark blue/silver with oxide red roof, as No.59102 'Village of Chantry' passes Fairwood with 7C31, the 09:45 Theale - Merehead stone empties.* (03/02)

(above) : *The former Foster Yeoman Class 59/0s have been repainted into their new owners (Aggregate Industries) livery of green, light grey and blue. There are five locos in the fleet, Nos.59001 - 59005, although No.59003 is now a GBRf loco. The first four locos were built in 1985, No.59005 in1989, all by General Motors at their plant at La Grange, Illinois, USA. The doyen member of the Class, No.59001 'Yeoman Endeavour' makes a splendid composition, as it heads along the Westbury Avoider with 7A09, the 07:12 Merehead - Acton Yard 'Jumbo' loaded stone. It is running several hours late and this may account why it only contains one portion.* (03/10)

Fairwood Junction

Fairwood Junction is accessed off Fairwood Road at the hamlet of Fairwood itself, down a track which leads to Little Fairwood farm. This is the point on the Reading - Taunton Line, west of Westbury, where the main line into Westbury Station and the Westbury Avoider converge. The road bridge above the junction offers views in both directions, but the view to the east has the added attraction of the Westbury White Horse on the hill above the town.

Fairwood Junction Signal Box used to be situated on the 'Up' side of the junction, a Type 28B structure, which opened in January 1933 with a 28 lever GW Vertical Tappet frame. The box closed in May 1984 when the new panel box at Westbury was commissioned.

(above) : *Class 59/0 No.59001 'Yeoman Endeavour' waits for the 13:06hrs London Paddington - Penzance HST to pass, before it can proceed with 7V16, the 11:47 Fareham - Whatley empty box wagons.* (06/09)

(below) : *Having been loaded with fresh ballast, the HOBC headed by FHH Class 66/5 No.66510 hurries towards the West of England main line with 6C73, the 13:12 Westbury - Fairwater Yard, Taunton.* (07/09)

(above) : *No.59001 'Yeoman Endeavour' is seen taking the Westbury station line at Fairwood Junction with 6A13, the 13:30 Whatley Quarry - West Drayton loaded stone conveyed in new IIA bogie stone hoppers, built in 2006 by Wagony Swidnica, Poland.* (07/09)

(below) : *On the same, very sunny and hot day, DBS cherry Red' livery Class 59/2 No.59206 'John F. Yeoman Rail Pioneer' takes the Westbury Avoider (aka the 'Westbury Cut-Off') with 7A17, the 10:31 Merehead - Acton Yard 'Jumbo' stone train, formed of two portions; 'MendipRail' IIA hoppers and JNA box wagons.* (07/09)

Westbury North Junction

(left) : *Class 59/0 No.59002 'Alan J Day' became the only member of the fleet to carry MendipRail colours of green, orange and silver, off-set by a large MRL and Mendip Rail branding midway along the bodyside.*

Here, the loco is seen at Westbury North Junction with 7V67, the10:33 Sevington - Merehead empty box wagons, having left the West of England main line at Heywood Road Junction. *(08/00)*

(below) : *Sporting Foster Yeoman livery of blue and silver with silver roof, Class 59/0 No.59004 'Paul A. Hammond' passes Westbury Panel signal box with 7C77, the 12:40 Acton Yard - Merehead empty 'Jumbo' stone train.*

In the days of mechanical signalling, Westbury must have been a very interesting place, lots of semaphore signals, plus the bonus of Class 52 'Western' hydraulic locos.

At one time, there used to be three signal boxes in the area: Westbury North, Westbury South and Westbury Middle signal box. *(03/10)*

Westbury 'Avoider'

(above) : *The line which avoids Westbury station runs for 2 miles and 37 chains between Heywood Road Jct. and Fairwood Jct..*

No.59206 'John F. Yeoman Rail Pioneer' is seen on the 'avoider' with the daily 7A17 'Jumbo' train, formed of loaded 'MendipRail' JNAs and IIAs bound for Acton Yard. *(09/09)*

Notable Landmarks

White Horse

(middle) : *The origin of the White Horse possibly commemorates King Alfred's victory at the Battle of Ethandun in 878. It is 180ft tall and 170ft wide, adopted as a symbol for the town of Westbury.*

Westbury Cement Works

(right) : *Westbury cement works was constructed in the early 1960s and mothballed in 2009, now only receiving cement in PCA tanks from Aberthaw.*

The 400ft chimney dominated the Wiltshire skyline for decades, until it was demolished in September 2016.

Background

Although this may not have been apparent after reading the first issue of 'Chasing Trains', as well as my passion for all things Class 40 and 50, I also like English Electric Class 37s. However, following my favourite classes of loco around the country, combined with work commitments, it was difficult, almost nigh on impossible, for me to devote time to these incredible locos.

The Class 37 became a familiar sight on the British Rail network, particularly when they were the main motive power for InterCity services in East Anglia and within Scotland, as well as a general freight work horse in all areas. They are versatile and, with common traction knowledge among train crew, the 37s could work pretty well anywhere.

They are now well over 60 years old and have become fondly known to railway enthusiasts as "Tractors", a nickname due to the agricultural sound of the loco's diesel engine. A total of 309 locos were built between 1960 - 1965.

Where Are They Now?

When I started to compile this edition in April 2020, there were still over 40 Class 37s in service, which amounted to 13% of the original 309 Class members, a fine testament to their durability, if not always their reliability in later years.

A note of where they all were on 1st April 2020 is given in *"Chasing Trains : Volume 3"*.

The end of Passenger Work

Later on you will see my exploits enjoying some haulage with 'Tractors' on both the Cumbrian Coast Line, plus the 'Wherry Lines' in East Anglia, and I am so glad that I made the effort to do so.

Why? .... after March 2020, for the first time in Class 37 history, there would be ***no Class 37-hauled diagrams*** for timetabled passenger services anywhere on the rail network; diagrams ended thus:

1st to go	:	January 2019	:	Carlisle - Barrow in Furness - Lancaster / Preston	(**DRS**)
2nd to go	:	May 2019	:	Norwich - Great Yarmouth / Lowestoft.	(**DRS**)
3rd to go	:	March 2020	:	Rhymney - Cardiff Central	(**COLAS**)

A 'Highland Fling'

In view of losing this 37-hauled activity, I thought a little digressing wouldn't go amiss and to recall a brief interlude I had with these venerable machines working, in particular, on the West Highland Line. This so called *'Highland Fling'*, which seems quite appropriate for a visit to Scotland, took place towards the end of the 1980s; three visits in all, although the last one in 1988 didn't start as rail-orientated - I was on holiday at the time - but, persistent bad weather put paid to my plans, so I actually spent some time travelling on the 37s. Fortuitous, one might say, I couldn't possibly comment!

11th May 1985

Travelling on the West Highland Line for the first time, came in May 1985, when I was in Oban, taking in one of the local landmarks - McCaig's Tower. The structure was commissioned by a wealthy, philanthropic, banker by the name of John Stuart McCaig. He was his own architect and the tower was erected between 1897 and his death on 29th June 1902; only the outer walls were constructed.

The structure sits prominently on Battery Hill, constructed from Bonawe granite and has a circumference of 656ft with two tiers of lancet arches, 44 on the lower level and 50 above. The height varies around the circumference as it takes account of the contours of the hill on which it stands. The views are breath-taking, overlooking the town itself, Oban Bay, the island of Kerrera and the Isle of Mull in the distance.

In fact, it was while I was taking in the view that I observed a Class 37 + a Class 20 at the station, coupling up to some Mk1 coaches, as if they were going to haul a train to Glasgow. I hurried down the hill and reached the station to investigate. The pair were indeed working to Glasgow and I bought a ticket for a short ride to Dalmally - the only time I enjoyed a Class 20 + Class 37 combination working in multiple and the sound was fantastic.The train was:

1T52, the 18:00 Oban - Glasgow Queen Street **Loco Nos.37051 + 20089**

Oban

(above) : *This was my view from McCaig's Tower in Oban, looking down towards the harbour, where two Caledonian Macbrayne ferries can be seen. The railway station had hosted a small rail gala; locos on show include three Class 37s, three Class 27s, a Class 20 and a Class 25 'Ethel' train heating unit. Ahead of an ex-works No.37188 is No.37051, which will collect the Class 20 and couple up to the rake of stock platformed on the left.*

(below) : *Class 37 No.37051 + Class 20 No.20189 wait to go with 1T52, the 18:00 Oban - Glasgow Queen Street.*

The West Highland Line

Where Is It?

The West Highland Line (WHL), which translates into Scottish Gaelic as 'Rathad Iarainn nan Eilean' - "Iron Road to the Isles" - is a railway that links the ports of Mallaig and Oban on the west coast of Scotland to Glasgow. I certainly believe it to be one of the most beautifully scenic railway lines in the world; in fact, in 2009, yhe line was voted by readers of the travel magazine 'Wanderlust' the top rail journey in the world, ahead of the Trans-Siberian Railway in Russia and the Cuzco to Machu Picchu line in Peru.

Construction

On 23rd October 1889, a silver spade cut the first sod in the construction of what would become the West Highland Railway, with work starting simultaneously between Arrochar, Crianlarich, Helensburgh and Tyndrum. The route was built in several sections:-

- Glasgow Queen Street to Cowlairs Junction.	(Edinburgh and Glasgow Railway)
- Cowlairs Junction to Bowling.	(Glasgow, Dumbarton and Helensburgh Railway)
- Bowling to Dumbarton Central.	(Lanarkshire and Dunbartonshire Railway)
- Dumbarton Central to Dalreoch.	(Caledonian and Dunbartonshire Junction Railway)
- Dalreoch to Craigendoran.	(Glasgow, Dumbarton and Helensburgh Railway)
- Craigendoran to Fort William.	(West Highland Railway)
- Crianlarich to Oban.	(Callander and Oban Railway)

The completed railway was approved by the Board of Trade on 3rd August 1894 and, four days later, the 100 miles of line was opened to passenger traffic between Craigendoran Junction and Fort William. Apparently, this was the greatest mileage of railway ever to be opened on one day in Britain!

There is also the 'Mallaig extension' ....

Oban (above) : *On the same day, after arriving in Oban, I observed Eastfield's Class 37/0 No.37188 looking absolutely sparkling after being named 'Jimmy Shand'. Sir James Shand MBE (28th January 1908 – 23rd December 2000) was a famous Scottish musician, who played traditional Scottish dance music on the accordion. His signature tune was "The Bluebell Polka".*

Craigendoran Junction (above) : *Split-headcode Class 37 No.37011 on 1T18, the 08:40 Fort William - Glasgow Queen Street comes off the WHL at Craigendoran Junction, where the line to Helensburgh Central diverges. The signal box closed in 1992, when control passed to Yoker Signalling Centre.* (11/05/85)

Mallaig Extension

On 1st April,1901, a 41¾ mile section was opened to Mallaig - known as the 'Mallaig Extension - and this completed the West Highland Railway. The line now technically starts from Fort William Junction (just under a mile out from Fort William station) and runs for a further 1 mile and 27 chains to Banavie Junction. Here, the mileage starts again, and Mallaig is reached 39½ miles later.

The station at Mallaig was laid out as an island platform with tracks on either side, sidings, plus a turntable to the south of the station, on the west side of the line. Until 1968, two tracks continued down onto the pier, but were removed when the harbour passed from British Rail ownership to that of the Mallaig Harbour Authority.

The whole line between Mallaig and Craigendoran Junction runs as single track.

Aesthetics

The railway passes through Glens and Bens, skirts many Lochs, all the way after leaving Craigendoran, plus the remoteness of inhospitable Rannoch Moor and the highest railway summit in Britain, Corrour - 1,350ft above sea level. As well as this there are some exceptional architectural features, as I found on my journeys - three, In fact, stand out:

1. *Horse Shoe Curve viaduct* : A girder viaduct is on a curve of 576ft consisting of nine spans of 60ft. on the Horseshoe Curve, south of Bridge of Orchy, under the mass of Ben Dorain (3,524ft).

2. *Glenfinnan viaduct* : A spectacular curving viaduct at the top of Loch Shiel, overlooking the Glenfinnan Monument, constructed by Sir Robert McAlpine, known as 'Concrete Bob'. The viaduct is built from mass concrete, has 21 semicircular spans of 50 feet, 416 yards long and crosses the River Finnan at a height of 100 feet. The viaduct is built on a curve of 792 feet.

3. *Loch nan Uamh viaduct* : The viaduct has eight concrete arches of 50 feet span, four each side of a large central concrete pylon, crossing the Allt a' Mhama, or Mama Burn, before it flows into Loch nan Uamh. The railway viaduct has a short tunnel at each end of the structure; Loch nan Uamh No.116 (66yds long) and No.117 (99yds) at the east and west end, respectively.

STOP

WEST HIGHLANDS

3rd - 7th December 1987

3 Dec 87							
37025	Euston	Mossend	391	1S07	2055	Euston	Fort William
4 Dec 87							
37405	Mossend	Glasgow Q. St	55¾	"	"	"	"
37412	Glasgow Q.St.	Fort William	122¾	"	"	"	"
37422	Fort William	Mallaig	41½	2Y51	1005	Fort William	Mallaig
37422	Mallaig	Fort William	41½	2Y54	1220	Mallaig	Fort William
37412	Fort William	Glasgow Q. St	122¾	1T34	1415	Fort William	Glasgow Q. St

5 Dec 87							
37403	Glasgow Q.St	Oban	101½	1Y11	0820	Glasgow Q.St.	Oban
37413	Oban	Crianlarich	42	1T44	1800	Oban	Glasgow Q. St
37425	Crianlarich	Glasgow Q. St	59¼	1T46	1550	Mallaig	Glasgow Q St
6 Dec 87							
47712	Glasgow Central	Edinburgh	53¼	1074	1100	Glasgow Q St	Edinburgh
47709	Edinburgh (via Cumbernauld)	Glasgow Central	53¼	1083	1530	Edinburgh	Glasgow Q St
7 Dec 87							
87015	Glasgow Central	Euston	401¼	1M20	0845	Ayr	Euston (Royal Scot)

Travel Log

9 Aug 88							
37424	Crianlarich	Arrochar	16¾	1T34	1445	Fort William	Glasgow
37423	Arrochar	Crianlarich	16¾	1Y15	1834	Glasgow	Oban
10 Aug 88							
37411	Crianlarich	Tulloch	45¾	1Y01	0347	Mossend	Fort William
37402	Tulloch	Crianlarich	45¾	1T18	0840	Fort William	Glasgow
37408	Crianlarich	Oban	42	1Y11	0834	Glasgow	Oban
37408	Oban	Crianlarich	42	1T28	1250	Oban	Glasgow
37423	Crianlarich	Tyndrum	5	1Y13	1204	Glasgow	Oban
37411	Tyndrum	Garelochhead	32¼	1T34	1445	Fort William	Glasgow
37409	Garelochhead	Crianlarich	27½	1Y23	1634	Glasgow	Fort William
11 Aug 88							
37422 / 37403	Crianlarich	Fort William	63 / 63	1Y01	0347	Mossend	Fort William
37422	Fort William	Mallaig	41½	2Y51	1005	Fort William	Mallaig
37422	Mallaig	Fort William	41½	2Y54	1230	Mallaig	Fort William
37403	Fort William	Arrochar	71¼	1T34	1445	Fort William	Glasgow
37424	Arrochar	Crianlarich	16¾	1Y23	1634	Glasgow	Fort William

(Previous pages)

(Page 148) : *Two Class 27s (Nos.27054 + 27206) wait at the rear of Eastfield MPD to take over a railtour, as Class 37/0 No.37026 'Loch Awe' heads past Cowlairs with 1T12, the 08:00 Oban - Glasgow Queen St..*

(Page 149) : *Stunning scenery, semaphore signals and a Class 37, what more could an enthusiast want? No.37037, now preserved at the South Devon Railway, pauses at Taynuilt for a westbound train to pass on 11th May 1985, while working 1T28, the 13:00 Oban - Glasgow Queen Street.*

WEST HIGHLANDS and the 'KYLE'

12th - 16th August 1988

12 Aug 88							
37425	Crianlarich	Glasgow	59¾	1T12	0810	Oban	Glasgow
37411	Glasgow	Rannoch	87¼	1Y23	1634	Glasgow	Fort William
37424	Rannoch	Crianlarich	28	1D15	1810	Fort William	Mossend
13 Aug 88							
37409	Crianlarich	Helensburgh	34¼	1T12	0810	Oban	Glasgow
37425	Helensburgh	Arrochar	17½	1Y21	1004	Glasgow	Fort William
37406	Arrochar	Dumbarton	26½	1T18	0840	Fort William	Glasgow
37409	Dumbarton	Tyndrum	48¼	1Y13	1204	Glasgow	Oban
37407 }	Tyndrum	Garelochhead	32¼	1T34	1445	Fort William	Glasgow
37422 }			32¼				
37405	Garelochhead	Crianlarich	27½	1Y23	1634	Glasgow	Fort William
15 Aug 88							
37419	Kyle of Lochalsh	Stromeferry	10¼	2H82	1128	Kyle of Lochalsh	Inverness
37417	Stromeferry	Kyle of Lochalsh	10¼	2H83	1010	Inverness	Kyle of Lochalsh
37414	Kyle of Lochalsh	Inverness	82¼	2H86	1505	Kyle of Lochalsh	Inverness
37415	Inverness	Kyle of Lochalsh	82¼	2H85	1820	Inverness	Kyle of Lochalsh
16 Aug 88							
37411	Fort William	Tulloch	17¾	1T18	0840	Fort William	Glasgow
37408 }	Tulloch	Fort William	17¾	1Y01	0347	Mossend	Fort William
37422 }			17¾				
37406	Fort William	Mallaig	41½	2Y51	1005	Fort William	Mallaig
37401	Mallaig	Fort William	41½	2Y58	1845	Mallaig	Fort William

Travel Log

FAR NORTH LINE

6th May 1983	37183	Inverness - Wick	161 miles 35 chains
	37262	Thurso - Georgemas Junction	6 miles 50 chains
	37183	Georgemas Junction - Inverness	147 miles 20 chains
30th September 1987		**"The Highlander" Landcruise**	
	37421	Inverness - Thurso	153 miles 70 chains
	37421	Thurso - Inverness	153 miles 70 chains
11th June 1988	37416	Inverness - Helmsdale	161 miles 35 chains
	37420	Helmsdale - Inverness	101 miles 40 chains

"The Iron Road to the Isles"

3rd - 7th December 1987

A birthday treat for me, in fact, the auspicious day falls on the 1st, but no matter. I had always wanted to complete a full run on the overnight sleeper from London Euston to Fort William, followed by a run on the 'Mallaig extension'. This was a memorable experience and the only time I experienced a sleeper on the West Coast Main Line.

3rd / 4th : I left Euston at five minutes to nine o'clock on the evening of 3rd December, hauled by my favourite class of electric locos, a Class 87 - No. 87025 'Borderer' - quite appropriate under the circumstances, as my train would indeed cross the Anglo-Scottish border at Gretna.

At the time, the train ran to Mossend Yard (Edinburgh today) where the electric loco was replaced by a Class 37/4 for the run over unelectrified lines to Fort William. The new loco was No.37405 'Strathclyde Region' which, due to operating constraints, went via Stirling to run round before returning south to Glasgow Queen Street, 55 miles later.

From Glasgow the 'Road to the Isles" would begin, with No.37412 'Loch Lomond' leading ....

To Crianlarich

After making our way out of the Glasgow suburbs along the north bank of the River Clyde, the first stop is Dumbarton, after which the line crosses the River Leven, which makes its way from Loch Lomond to the Clyde. Upon reaching Craigendoran Junction, a single line diverges to Helensburgh Central while my train moves onto the West Highland line proper and 100 miles to go before reaching Fort William.

From here it is a series of lochs and mountains and, apart from a few dips along the way, it's a steady climb all the way to the first summit at Glen Douglas (564ft), from where the train driver applies some brakes to steady the train down a grade of 1 in 57 to reach Arrochar & Tarbet, the gateway to Loch Lomond - the biggest body of inland water in Britain. A little further on and I could see Inversnaid Hotel on the north bank of the Loch, from where tourists to and from the Trossachs transfer between the Loch Lomond steamer 'Maid of the Loch' and the Stronachlachar coach.

The line hugs the shoreline of this loch as far as Ardlui, after which the territory passes from Argyll & Bute into Perthshire, crossing Glen Falloch Viaduct to pass through beautiful (a term used frequently out of necessity!) Glen Falloch. The railway shares this passage with both the River Falloch and A82 road to reach Crianlarich.

I must say that the views are breathtaking, a clear blue sky, with snow capped mountains and, as the sun rises, I enjoy a cup of coffee from a comfortable seat in a day coach.

On arriving in Crianlarich. I am surrounded by mountains - Ben More (3,843ft), Ben Lui (3,708ft), Ben Oss (3,374ft) and Ben Dhu Craig (3,024ft).

Five miles out of Crianlarich, the line to Oban via Tyndrum Lower diverges, while we continue northwards on the WHL via Tyndrum Upper on a steady climb for seven miles to reach the second highest summit on the WHL - County March at 1,024ft above sea level.

I could see the conical mass of Ben Dorain (3,524ft.) in the distance *(inset)* - a truly impressive sight and I could just make out the railway as it made its way around the base.

The train now runs along the side of Ben Odhar to approach the famous horseshoe curve, then goes round Ben Odhar, across a viaduct to the foot of Beinn A Chaistel, then by a viaduct again to the mighty Ben Dorain. So, effectively, the line doubles back on itself in the form of a horseshoe.

Inhospitable Rannoch Moor

After Bridge of Orchy, the line passes through Achallader and as I look through the carriage window, the ruin of a castle of the same name appears on my left; the train now climbing steadily by the side of the Water of Tulla below me. The terrain is becoming decidedly bleak as train 1S07 edges steadily northwards onto Rannoch Moor; a moor which is over 20 miles long and 20 miles wide.

When the West Highland Line was built across Rannoch Moor, its builders had to float the tracks on a mattress of tree roots, brushwood and thousands of tons of earth and ashes to prevent the heavy steel tracks sinking in the bog. Rannoch station opened to passengers on 7 August 1894 and now comprises a crossing loop and an island platform.

Generally, the station is served by three trains per day in each direction between Glasgow Queen Street and Fort William / Mallaig, a fourth, if you count the Caledonian Sleeper.

As I leave Rannoch station behind me, I start to see why the Moor is so barren and inhospitable, I could see some old snow fences protecting the line, before the line passes through Cruach Snowshed - the only one in Britain to protect the cutting from continual snowdrifts, which prevail here during the winter months.

I reach Corrour, 1,350ft above sea level *(inset)*, the summit of the WHL - a windswept place, which marks the end of Rannoch Moor.

Initially, the station was only provided for railway workers and their families but, in the early twentieth century, the station saw more use by an influx of navvies working on hydro-electric schemes and aluminium works. Although their lodgings were in the small village of Kinlochleven, some 10-miles away, its access was remote, resulting in a long, hard, walk across peat bogs to reach the station.

Through Glen Spean

Leaving Corrour behind, as it was a clear day, I glimpsed my fist view of Ben Nevis, the highest mountain in Britain at 4,406ft high, north west of here as the line skirts Loch Treig. The WHL drops away from Corrour through Tulloch all the way to Fort William, the scenery changes dramatically from barren moorland to lush, fertile, grasslands of the Spean Valley.

As long as you do not stop looking out of the carriage window, you will be rewarded with an another spectacular view as the train passes through the Monessie Gorge. The valley narrows and both the railway and the River Spean pass through the gorge, which is now on the left below the level of the track. The water rushes, foams and cascades over the rocks and boulders, thrusting its way through the narrow gully until forcing its way to wider banks beyond.

At Spean Bridge, the River Spean diverges right and actually courses the route of the old Fort Augustus Railway and when you look to the right, there is a monument on a hill, which is a memorial to the commandos who were trained near Spean Bridge during World War II.

Into Fort William.

Nearing Fort William, I notice the remains of Old Inverlochy Castle, a 13th century stronghold which was last fought over in 1645 when an army of clansmen failed in their attempt to capture the castle from the Royalists. Inverlochy is now a ruin, but is unusual because it has remained unaltered since it was built in the reign of King Alexander III.

Just over half-a-mile out of Fort William my train approaches Mallaig Junction, where the line from Mallaig joins the WHL into Fort William - there is no direct line from Mallaig onto the WHL south from here. In the vee of the two lines is Banavie Junction signal box (as originally named) opened in August 1894 and remains operational today. It has been renamed twice during its existence, in line with the junction itself, the present lever frame of 30 levers, dates from 1973.

So, 569 miles and 12 hours later, I arrive in Fort William, ready for the next leg to Mallaig.

4th December 1987

The 'Mallaig Extension'

After arriving in Fort William, the train engine, No.37412, would lay over at Fort William depot before working to Glasgow Queen Street at 14:15hrs in the afternoon, which would be my train south.

In the meantime, I was off to Mallaig to complete the West Highland Line in its entirety - just another 42 miles or so. My train was formed of three coaches, hauled by another Class 37/4 loco, No.37422, which would be the same combination on the return working.

Banavie

At this point, the railway crosses the River Lochy - part of the Caledonian Canal which runs from Fort William to Inverness. As I look to my right, I can see 'Neptune's Staircase', a series of locks which give access to the higher levels of the canal.

Banavie is also the centre for the line's Radio Electronic Token Block (RETB) signalling system, which replaced manual tokens handed from signalman to train driver - this resulted in signal boxes and semaphore signals being decommissioned between Mallaig and Helensburgh Upper.

As my train left Banavie, passing the paper mills at Corpach, we skirt the shoreline of Loch Eil, well known for outward bound activities, I looked back to see an impressive view of Ben Nevis which, would you believe, has a circumference of 24 miles around its base!

Glenfinnan

A truly great vista greets my eye as the train nears Glenfinnan, the 100ft high Glenfinnan Viaduct , one of the most photographed structures in Scotland, not to mention its role in the Harry Potter movies, with the 'Hogwarts Express' filmed crossing the viaduct. As my train too crosses the viaduct, there are spectacular views of Loch Shiel and the Bonnie Prince Charlie monument below, which marks the spot where Charles Edward Stuart unfurled his standard in 1745. If only the train could pause here for a moment, so passengers could take it all in!

The railway then curves into Glenfinnan station through a rocky cutting that was the source of much of the material used in the construction of the viaduct.

The Tunnels

For much of the WHL, the railway skirts the shoreline of lochs and crosses inhospitable moorland and peat bog, but on the Mallaig Extension, between Glenfinnan and Arisaig, the railway passes through rocky outcrops, which required a different solution - tunnels - and no less than 10 in a stunning 18-mile stretch:

- Leachabhuidh Tunnels	No. 77	(88yds)	No.78	(66yds)
- Lochailort Tunnel	No.102	(176yds)		
- Polnish Tunnels	No.106	(38yds)	No.107	(44yds)
- Loch nan Uamh Tunnels	No.116	(66yds)	No.117	(99yds)
- Beasdale Tunnels	No.118	(192yds)	No.119	(154yds)
- Borrodale Tunnel		(350yds)		

Whilst Glenfinnan Viaduct receives most of the plaudits, many consider the viaduct between the two Loch nan Uamh tunnels the best. As I crossed it, I had my first view of the Atlantic ocean.

Seven miles later and I had arrived in Mallaig.

Mallaig

Mallaig is the main commercial fishing port on the West Coast of Scotland and, during the 1960s, was the busiest herring port in Europe, priding itself on its famous traditionally smoked kippers.

The village was founded in the 1840s, when Lord Lovat of the North Morar Estate, divided up the farm of Mallaigvaig into 17 tracts of land and encouraged his tenants to move to the western part of the peninsula and turn to fishing as a way of life.

In the summer months, the special 'Jacobite' steam excursion runs daily between Fort William and Mallaig which brings in passengers from all over the world, including me, once!

MALLAIG

(above) : *The Class 37 has run round the three coach formation after arriving at Mallaig and No.37422 now waits to leave with 2Y54, the 12:20 Mallaig - Fort William.*

The train will stop at all stations en route, except Beasdale. Beasdale only sees one train a day in each direction.

(middle) : *After landing their catch, fishing vessels moor up in gorgeous winter sunshine, the crew take a well-earned rest, before sailing off later in the day for the next catch.*

(right) : **"The Jacobite"**

No.62005, now preserved, spends most of its time on the summer Fort William - Mallaig 'Jacobite' service (as No.2005) and she is seen here after arriving at Mallaig. The loco is sporting LNER apple green, a livery it never carried when in service.

The heavy gradients of the West Highland Line demanded powerful locos and the London and North Eastern Railway K1 Class, 2-6-0 steam loco fitted the bill. (19/09/87)

5th December 1987

Interlude

On **Sunday, the 5th**, I had an enforced break from the West Highland Line as there was no Sunday service between Glasgow and Fort William / Mallaig. So I had a day out in Edinburgh instead.

As my hotel was close to Glasgow Central, I decided to travel to the Scottish Capital from Central station, which was timetabled via Shotts.

However, due to engineering work, the normal route was blocked and my train was diverted via:

- Rutherglen East Junction,
- Carmyle,
- Coatbridge Central,
- Cumbernauld,
- Greenhill Lower Junction,
- Falkirk Grahamston,
- Polmont
- Haymarket

.... a longer, but more interesting route.

(above) : *Whilst at Glasgow Central, Class 37/0 No.37023 is seen making its way out of the station. .*

6th December 1987

Oban

After an early breakfast, I left my hotel and made the short walk to Glasgow Queen Street station to catch the train to Oban, which was:

Train : 1Y11, the 08:20 Glasgow Queen Street - Oban
Loco : No.37403 'Isle of Mull'

No.37403 bursts into life, the engine throbbing nicely, passing through Queen Street High Level Tunnel, the driver piling on the power to make sure his train gets up the 1 in 45 climb to reach level ground at Cowlairs, 1 mile and 25 chains later. From here, the loco takes the North Curve, onto the Maryhill line and through the Glasgow suburbs on the north bank of the River Clyde.

At Craigendoran Junction, the electrified lines are left behind and I retrace the route to Crianlarich, as described earlier on page 152.

Shortly after leaving Crianlarich, a lower line diverges for Oban. As I do so, I can see the Fort William line steadily climbing at a gradient of 1 in 60 through Tyndrum Upper to reach County March Summit at 1,024ft. Meanwhile, as my train climbs through the valley of Fillan Water, to reach Lower Tyndrum, the summit of this line is reached at 840ft - a mere 184ft lower than the other summit.

The line now travels through Argyllshire, after leaving Perthshire, and the beauty of Glen Lochy to reach Dalmally, shortly after which the ruins of Kilchurn Castle can be seen - an ancient stronghold of the Clan Campbell. The line sweeps round the head of Loch Awe and enters the Pass of Brander where Ben Cruachan stands tall (3,689ft) on my right-handside - Class 37/4 No.37404 was named after this mountain in January 1986.

I also noted wire fencing in the pass to safeguard against landslides and rocks falling on the line; in the event of this happening, the wire will trigger signals to danger. Moving swiftly through Taynuilt and Connel Ferry and Loch Etive, the line passes through Glen Cruitten.

I reach Oban, 101 miles after leaving Glasgow Queen Street.

GLASGOW QUEEN STREET

(above) : *The driver of No.37411 'The Institution of Railway Signal Engineers' opens up the throttle, throwing up plumes of black exhaust, to ascend the incine to Cowlairs and then on to Eastfield MPD.*

OBAN

(below) : *Class 37/4 No.37403 'Isle of Mull' is seen at Oban in the process of running round the stock, after arriving with 1Y11, the 08:20 glasgow Queen Street - Oban. No.37412 'Strathclyde Region' is stabled in the background and McCaig's Tower sits proudly on the hillside.*

GALLERY OF 37/4s

9th - 16th August 1988

This was intended to be a week touring the West Highlands, supposedly in the height of summer with clear blue skies and abundant sunshine. However, I was forgetting that this is one of the wettest parts of the UK where, for the time of year, the average temperature is only 64^0F with 5 inches of rainfall.

Sure enough, it rained every day, totally dull and miserable, feeling decidedly cool too. So, I spent most of the time on the trains and here is a selection of images as a record of my travels.

Fort William (1) : *On the morning of 16th August, No.37411 'The Institution of Railway Signal Engineers' sits patiently at Platform 2 ready to depart with 1T18, the 08:40 Fort William - Glasgow Queen Street.*

Tulloch (2) : *Whilst waiting for my train, I got a quick record shot of No.37409 'Loch Awe', gently ticking over in the Up Refuge Siding (used by the civil engineers) on a short rake of 'Sealion' hoppers loaded with ballast.*

(3) : *I had actually made an early start on 16th August, travelling from Fort William with No37411 'The Institution of Railway Signal Engineers' on 1T18, as far as Tulloch to await 1Y01, the 03:347 Mossend - Fort William. This is a portion of the overnight sleeper from London Euston and Nos.37408 'Loch Rannoch' + 37422 are seen pulling into Tulloch with 1Y01, which I took to Fort William.*

Upper Tyndrum (4) : *There were only a handful of daylight-hour freight services on the WHL and I was always pleased to be in a position to take a photograph, usually when a freight train paused at one of the many island platforms for pathing purposes. With a meagre consist of five Railfreight vans, No.37406 'The Saltire Society' waits to proceed with 7Y37, the 11:52 Mossend - Corpach 'Speedlink' service.*

Upper Tyndrum (above) : *"It's a pair" .... something I always looked forward to on the WHL, double-heading was a common practice to reposition locos, thus avoiding costly light engine movements between Glasgow and Fort William. Here, Nos.37411 'The Institution of Railway Signal Engineers' + No.37412 'Loch Lomond' enter Upper Tyndrum with 1T34, the 14:45 Fort William - Glasgow Queen Street.*

Arrochar and Tarbet (below) : *The station building at Arrochar and Tarbet station is available 'To Let', presumably there will be takers considering its close proximity to Loch Lomond. Here, No.37423 'Sir Murray Morrison' waits at Arrochar with 1Y15, the 18:34 Glasgow Queen Street - Oban. The 37 sports two-tone grey railfreight livery with blue & yellow chevrons representing its allocation to the metals and automotive sector.*

The Road to the Kyle

15th August 1988

This was day 7 of what had been a miserable week of bad weather. The saving grace was that I could ride the 37s on the West Highland Line, which was truly impressive, especially as some services were double-headed, two locos working in multiple.

However, on the 15th, I decided to have a break from these services and drive to the Kyle of Lochalsh and do an out & back run to Inverness. This would not be my first visit to the Kyle, which I had done on two previous occasions, both charter trains:

12th May 1984	:	Nos.26021 + 26038
1st October 1987	:	No.37417

The Drive

The other alternative to travel on the line to the Kyle was by train from Glasgow Queen Street via Inverness, which I discounted as being too time consuming, probably a 5-6 hour journey, combined with the difficulty of getting back to Crianlarich later in the day.

So, I opted for the most practical solution - drive to the Kyle of Lochalsh and train from there - a car journey of about 126 miles, taking two and a half hours, but the scenery was magnificent, seeing the West Highlands in a different perspective than being on the train.

I remember going over Rannoch Moor and passing through Glen Coe; the glen is U-shaped, formed by an ice age glacier, just under eight miles long, narrowing sharply at the 'Pass of Glen Coe'. I approached from the east on the A82, below the foot of Buachaille Etive Beag, passing tumbling waterfalls on my way through the pass, following the flow of water to the small Loch Achtriochtan.

The south side of the glen is marked by a succession of distinct volcanic peaks: passing Buachaille Etive Beag first, followed by the famous 'Three Sisters' (Beinn Fhada, Gearr Aonach, and Aonach Dubh), three steeply-sided ridges that extend north into the Glen. Emerging from the pass, the A82 proceeds through Fort William, along the shores of Loch Lochy, to Invergarry, where I leave the A82 for the A87 all the way to the Kyle of Lochalsh.

As I arrive, Class 37/4 No.37419 was waiting to leave with the 11:28hrs service for Inverness.

Loch Lochy

(above) : *Rain clouds hover menacingly over the mountains on the west bank of Loch Lochy, with snow-clad peaks and the tree line clearly visible. The loch is nine miles long and has an average depth of 230ft, being the third deepest loch of Scotland. It is located 10 miles south west of Loch Ness along the Great Glen.*

The Trains

To maximise the number of 37s I could ride behind today, I started off with No.37419, but only as far as Stromeferry, to meet the 10:10hrs service (2H83) arriving from Inverness, which turned out to be No.37417 'Highland Region'.

Back at the Kyle, it was to be No.37414 for my run to Inverness, the Highland Capital.

The Line ....

itself, runs as a single track railway line from the Kyle of Lochalsh to Dingwall, where it joins the 'Far North' line from Inverness to Wick and Thurso. The route was built in three sections:

- Inverness and Dingwall	Inverness and Ross-shire Railway	(Opening, October 1864)
- Dingwall and Stromeferry	Dingwall and Skye Railway	(Opening, August 1870)
- Kyle of Lochalsh Extension	(Highland Railway)	(Opening, November 1897)

The Strathpeffer Branch operated between 1885 and 1951.

In 1933, the London, Midland and Scottish Railway introduced two named trains on the line, 'The Hebridean' and 'The Lewisman'.

There are 11 stations on the route after leaving Dingwall, some of which have magical names, if not difficult to pronounce: Lochluichart, Achanalt, Achnasheen and Achnashellach. Only Garve, Achnasheen and Strathcarron have two platforms, all the rest have only one, and all are unstaffed.

The Route (from east to west - Inverness to Kyle of Lochalsh)

This is, in my opinion, completely different to that of the West Highland line; a more pastoral landscape, in the shadows of mountains and forests, beside bright lochs and wide open moors. The Kyle line is basically an arc which runs 'coast to coast', east to west, from Inverness on the Moray Firth to the Kyle of Lochalsh on Loch Alsh and the Inner Sound.

Between Dingwall and Garve, the line climbs at 1 in 50 to reach its first summit - Ravens Rock at 458ft - before descending at 1 in 50 to Garve. After leaving Garve the line runs parallel with the A890 road to the Kyle and, as the train headed further west, I noticed herds of deer on the hillside - a magnificent sight and the first time I had seen Highland Stags in the wild. The train had now passed the third highest point on the line - Corriemuille, at 429ft.

The line sweeps past Loch Luichart and Loch Chuilinn, coursing the River Bran before reaching Achnasheen, considered to be the half way point of my journey, although technically the half way point is at Luib Summit (646ft), 31 miles and 40 chains out of Dingwall.

Continuing ever westward, as I look out of the window I can see the Torridon Hills, just before the train stops at Achnashellach, among the most dramatic and spectacular peaks in the British Isles, many are over 3,000ft, so are considered 'Munros'.

As the train travels the remaining 18 miles to the Kyle, the line skirts beautiful Loch Carron, a sea loch on the west coast of Ross and Cromarty, which separates the Lochalsh Peninsula from the Applecross Peninsula. It is the point at which the River Carron enters the North Atlantic Ocean.

Nearing the end of my three-hour journey, I am rewarded with my first sight of the Isle of Skye and the ferry waiting to carry both residents and tourists across the Kyle Akin strait to Kyleakin. Nowadays, a new suspension bridge spans the strait, opened in 1995, taking the A87 road all the way to Uig in the north of the isle of Skye.

Kyle of Lochalsh (above) : *With the Isle of Skye in the background, No.37414 waits to leave 'the Kyle' with 2H86, the 15:05 Kyle of Lochalsh - Inverness, formed of four vehicles. One of these is a 'BG' (Brake Gangwayed) coach which has a guard's compartment in the centre and two large areas either side for storing luggage. This means that this particular formation only has 2½ coaches available for seating, but I was only going as far as Stromeferry..*

INVERNESS (below) : *For my return journey to the 'Kyle', No.47415 is in charge of the 18:20hrs service to the Kyle of Lochalsh, reporting code 2H85, which is seen at Platform 5. Due to the fact I would not be arriving back in Fort William until around 22:30hrs, I decided to spend the night there instead of driving all the way to Crianlarich.*

Three 37s on the Kyle

Stromeferry (above) : *Stromeferry was the original terminus of the Dingwall and Skye Railway which opened in 1870, where trains connected with steamer services from the pier to the islands of Skye. The present station is just a single platform with little in the way of passenger amenities. No.47417 'Highland Region' pulls into the station with 2H83, the 10:10 Inverness - Kyle of Lochalsh; I was the only one waiting to catch the train!*

(above) : **No.37417**	Introduced : 02/65	First Depot : 86A Cardiff Canton	
Numbers : D6969 (new) / 37269 / (02/74) / 37417 (11/85)		Fate : Withdrawn (12/12)	Cut Up

(top left) : **No.37414**	Introduced : 06/65	First Depot : 86A Cardiff Canton	
Numbers : D69873 (new) / 37287 (05/74) / 37414 (11/85)		Fate : Withdrawn (10/05)	Cut Up

(left) : **No.37415**	Introduced : 04/65	First Depot : 86A Cardiff Canton	
Numbers : D6977 (new) / 37277 / (05/74) / 37415 (11/85)		Fate : Withdrawn (12/09)	Cut Up

'On Shed'

Inverness MPD

(above) : **No.37033** *is one of five Class 37s stabled during the weekend in between duties at Inverness. Behind N.37033 are Nos.37157, 37109, an unidentified 37 and 37260. As was common amongst Scottish 37s, many were fitted with a central headlight and mini snow ploughs.*

Details for No.37033 can be found on Page168.

(above) : **No.37420**	Introduced : 07/65	First Depot	: 86A Cardiff Canton		
Numbers : D6997 (new) / 37297 (05/74) / 37420 (12/85)		Fate	: Withdrawn (09/07)	Cut Up	

Inverness

Depot Location

The depot sits to the north of Inverness station, within a triangle bounded by:

Rose Street Junction
Inverness Station
Welsh's Bridge Junction

The Rose Street Curve between Welsh's Bridge Junction and Rose Street Junction gives passenger and freight traffic direct access to the Kyle of Lochalsh and Far North Lines. This is especially useful for long trains, such as pipe trains from the Hartlepool Pipe Mill, destined for use in the North Sea oil and gas industry.

Inverness's famous horse shoe shaped engine shed, whose turntable was reached through a triumphal water tank-bearing archway, closed in 1962. In the diesel era, Inverness was the first depot in Scotland (1960) to receive BR / Sulzer Type 2's (Class 24) from Derby Works, to work alongside BRCW Type 2's (Class 26) and oust steam from the Highlands.

The 24s were numbered D5114–D5132 and, as they were coded 'Blue Star' for working in multiple, they often interchanged with the depot's Class 26s, which also had a 'Blue Star' rating.

The locos were later fitted with tablet catcher equipment on the side of the cab, used on single lines, which could be extended just before the train passed the exchange point and automatically retracted clear after the actual exchange. This was for use on single line sections and removed the need for a loco to stop and the driver exchange the token with the signalman.

Initially, Inverness was allocated a shed code of 60A by British Railway, with sub-sheds at Dingwall, Fortrose and Kyle of Lochalsh before becoming simply IS under TOPS.

In the 1980s, the depot adopted the Highland Stag as its emblem (*inset*) and, even after some locos were transferred to other depots, the emblem could still be seen under the cab.

The Station

Inverness station opened on 5th November 1855, the western terminus of the Inverness and Nairn Railway designed by architect, Joseph Mitchell.

It comprised a single covered passenger platform 200ft in length with three lines of rails, one each for arrivals, departures, and a spare line for carriages.

The terminus station is at one apex of a triangular junction in the centre of Inverness, with each half of the station connected to one line. One aspect of the layout is similar to Perth station, where separate platforms serve different routes. In the case of Inverness:

- Platforms 1 to 4 : The Highland Main and Aberdeen Line.
- Platform 5 to 7 : The Far North Line and the Kyle of Lochalsh.

  NB. Platform 5 also has access to the east, but only for a short train (eg. two vehicles).

I recall being able to walk from the end of Platform 6 and enter the grounds of Inverness MPD; there always seemed to be a friendly Depot Foreman on duty who allowed me to look round, jot down the locos 'on shed' and take photographs. I remember thinking at the time, Inverness was probably the most welcoming of all the depots I visited.

The Far North Line

Inverness - Wick / Thurso

Setting The Scene

The Far North Line is another rural railway line entirely within the Highland region, running from Inverness to Wick and Thurso, the northernmost railway in the United Kingdom. In common with other rural lines in Scotland, the majority is single track, especially north of Dingwall. All trains are diesel-powered.

The line is the longest railway in Scotland and the mileages from Inverness are:

Wick : 161 miles and 35 chains

Thurso : 153 miles and 46 chains

The Far North Line runs directly to Wick, but trains to Thurso have to reverse at Georgemas Junction, which is a branch 6 miles and 54 chains in length. At the time I visited the area in 1983, through passenger services between Inverness and Wick completed the journey in four hours, stopping at all stations, including a Thurso portion being attached / detached at Georgemas Junction.

For much of the way, after Dingwall, the Far North Line generally follows the line of the Moray Firth coastline, except when the line sweeps inland between:

Argay - Lairg - Golspie

Helmsdale - Georgemas Junction - Wick

Personal Perspective

I have travelled on the far North Line on three occasions (1983, 1987 and 1988) all involving Class 37 traction, but that was the main attraction for me, as I found the line uninspiring, although it did enable me to visit n John O'Groats and Dunnet's head, the northernmost point on mainland Britain.

The two images here are taken from a trip to Thurso when I was invited by British Rail InterCity to sample a 'wine & dine' luxury landcruise - 'The Highlander'.

THURSO

(left) : *Class 37/0 No.37261' Caithness' is seen at Thurso waiting to leave with a three coach train formed of two Mk1 coaches and a 'BG'.*

This is a 'portion' for Georgemas Junction, where it will be attached to the main train from Wick to Inverness.

The train alongside is 'The Highlander' landcruise charter, bound for Inverness. Interestingly, the loco ran round at Georgemas junction in order to continue south - a fresh Class 37 loco would have been nice but, I suppose, this would be cost-prohibitive!

(left) : *Close up shot of No.37421 at Thurso on 'The Highlander'.*

The details for No.37421 are:

- *New in February 1965 as No.D6967.*
- *Allocated to (41A).*
- *Became No.37267 under TOPS.*
- *No.37421 from December 1985.*
- *Currently operational for Colas rail.*

Eastfield MPD, Glasgow

A Little History

There has been a shed / depot of sorts on this site since 1904, situated in the area of Springburn, Glasgow, made up of generally working class households in large sandstone built tenement blocks.

The area has historically been linked to the railways and there were four main railway sites located in Springburn:

- North British Railway's Cowlairs Works in 1841.
- Caledonian Railway's St Rollox Works in 1856.
- Neilson and Company's Hyde Park Works in 1861.
- Sharp Stewart and Company's Atlas Works in 1888.
- North British Railway's Eastfield shed in 1904.

Eastfield

1904 - 1973

The engine shed at Eastfield opened in 1904 on what was the Edinburgh and Glasgow Railway and replaced Cowlairs shed, which closed. It came about after the opening of the Glasgow, Dumbarton and Helensburgh Railway.

Although the shed could only be accessed from the south, it was doubled ended, which meant steam engines could pass through the entire shed. British Railways allocated the shed 65A and there were a number of sub-sheds in its area of control:

Aberfoyle / Helensburgh / Kilsyth / Kipps / Lennoxtown / Motherwell / Parkhead / Polmadie

1973 - 1993

Eastfield was re-coded 'ED' under TOPS and, at the time of my visit, had a large allocation of diesel locos:

- Type 1 : Class 20
- Type 2 : Class 24 / 25 / 27
- Type 3 : Class 37
- Type 4 : Class 47

There was also a number of Class 06 (0-4-0) and Class 08 (0-6-0) shunting locos, but no Type 5s, like the legendary Class 55 'Deltics'.

Just like other depots, Eastfield adopted a logo / mascot, which was applied to the bodyside of its locos in the form of a 'Scottie' dog. However, it resembled more a 'Westie', a West Highland Terrier, which would be appropriate considering the depot's association with the West Highland Line.

The depot itself was situated on the 'Down' side of the main running lines serving Glasgow Queen Street station between Cowlairs East Junction and Cowlairs West Junction. Traffic for the West Highland Line would use the 'North Curve' between Cowlairs North and West Junctions.

Due to the end of loco-hauled passenger trains running out of Glasgow Queen Street, combined with a general downturn in freight, Eastfield's importance diminished and it closed. The remaining diesel locos were re-allocated to other depots and the track was lifted in 1994.

2005 to date

A new, but much smaller, depot opened in 2005 to service Scotrail Class 158 and Class 170 DMUs, partly to ease overcrowding at Edinburgh Haymarket.

(above) : **No.37033** Introduced : 03/62 First Depot : 50B Hull Dairycoates
Numbers : D6733 (new) / 37033 / (10/73) / 37719 (03/89) Fate : Withdrawn (09/07) Cut Up

(above) : **No.37021** Introduced : 07/61 First Depot : 32A Norwich
Numbers : D6721 (new) / 37021 (02/74) / 37715 (08/88) Fate : Withdrawn (06/99) Cut Up

'On Shed'

Eastfield MPD

(above) : **No.37085**
Introduced : 12/62
First Depot : 52A Gateshead
Numbers : D6785 (new)
37085 (03/74)
37711 (06/88)
Fate : Withdrawn (12/99)
Cut Up

(middle) : **No.37264**
Introduced : 01/65
First Depot : 41A Tinsley
Numbers : D6964 (new)
37264 (01/74)
Fate : Preserved

(right) : **No.37405**
Introduced : 05/65
First Depot : 86A Cardiff Canton
Numbers : D6982 (new)
37282 (03/74)
37405 (05/85)
Fate : Operational

No.37422 at Ardlui om 7D10, the 06:05 Fort William - Mossend

No.37423 at Eastfield MPD

Background

It was 2010, and I was casually looking back over my old haulage records and, to my astonishment, 20 years had elapsed since I last went out 'bashing' (ie. a term, enthusiasts coined for travelling behind different locos) - Spring Bank Holiday, Monday, 28th May 1990, to be precise. On that day a Class 50 had the honour of being the final run in the shape of No.50024 'Vanguard' working 1F45, the 11:00 Oxford - London Paddington.

How I missed this activity, no more Class 40s whistling merrily away along the North Wales Coast on a Summer Saturday-dated holiday service, a 'Peak' on the North East/South West route or a 50 on the West of England Main Line to Penzance.

Those days were long gone and loco-hauled travel was sparse, to say the least. There were pockets around the network, but these mainly related to overnight sleeper services, notably Class 37s/67s working sleeper 'portions' on the non-electrified routes in Scotland. National Express operated Class 90 hauled trains on the London - Norwich route, but these were not to everyone's liking.

Of course, the loss of Class 47/8s and 86s/87s on Virgin West Coast / Cross Country services eight years previously left a huge hole for enthusiasts. Fortunately, it was not all doom and gloom and as I was to find out in the forthcoming years, loco-hauled trains would make a revival, starting with ....

WSMR

Wrexham, Shropshire and Marylebone Railway .... an open access operator, started running passenger services between Wrexham and London Marylebone from April 2008 until the Company's demise in 2011.

Services were operated by an ESWR (English, Scottish & Welsh Railway / later D B Schenker) Class 67, Mk3 carriages and DVT (Driving Van Trailer). Initially, until the DVTs and Mk3s came on stream, Mk3s were hired in from Cargo-D and operated in top and tail mode with a Class 67 at each end. Five trains ran in each direction each weekday.

By the time I sampled this service, the operation was in full swing - Class 67 + Mk3s + DVT - all in corporate livery, the 67 in half light grey and dark grey halves with 'Wrexham & Shropshire' branding.

Banbury (above) : *Unfortunately, the day did not start well, dull and overcast conditions greeted the arrival of Class 67 No.67014 'Thomas Telford', which is seen approaching Banbury on 3rd August 2010 with 1J82, the 11:20 London Marylebone - Wrexham. All aboard, and No.67014 was routed through the West Midlands via Bordesley, Birmingham New Street, Soho South Junction, Bescott, Portobello Junction and Wolverhampton.*

Shrewsbury (opposite) : *My train approached Shrewsbury via Severn Bridge Junction, just south of the station, which is controlled by the largest operational mechanical signal box in the world. Its LNWR origin dates back to 1876 and has three storeys, two built of red brick and cement and a third floor mainly of wooden weather board pin-panel containing the glass windows. The roof is Welsh slate. The main operational floor houses a 180 lever interlocking frame, about half of these are now in use.*

The Route

From Wrexham General, services ran via:

Ruabon / Chirk / Gobowen / Shrewsbury / Wellington / Telford / Cosford / Wolverhampton to Tame Parkway, from there non-stop to Banbury, via either Stetchford, Birmingham International and Coventry, or via Birmingham New Street and Solihull.

Due to competition agreements held by other TOCs, WSMR could not call at Birmingham New Street or Coventry. Furthermore, to protect Chiltern Railways, northbound services could only pick up and southbound services set down at Banbury. From December 2009, the Banbury restrictions were lifted and services also called at Leamington Spa.

A Day Out

3rd August 2010, proved to be the only time I sampled a WSMR service to Shrewsbury and Wrexham, each way from Banbury. Living in Swindon, Banbury was the easiest point at which I could board a WSMR train. I had considered going by train, but this necessitated a change at both Didcot Parkway and Oxford, which was not appealing. So, along with my friend Graham, we drove to Banbury instead.

WSMR Demise

In the end, low passenger numbers and operating restrictions made it difficult for WSMR to survive. On 28th January 2011, operations ceased after concluding there was no prospect of the business ever being profitable and the rolling stock was transferred to Chiltern Railways.

So, goodbye WSMR, hello Chiltern Trains, who have since gone from strength to strength, first with Class 67s and now Class 68s, hired-in from DRS.

Chiltern Railways

From 13th December 2010, Chiltern Railways commence running loco-hauled services; 2 diagrams initially, to increase capacity on the Chiltern Line into London Marylebone, plus to provide cover whilst the Class 165 units are fitted with GSM-R equipment.

The diagrams, for use on peak-time, commuter, services are:

(1) 1H06, 05:54 Birmingham Moor St. - London Marylebone
1R47, 16:33 London Marylebone - Birmingham Moor St.

(2) 1H08, 06:53 Banbury - London Marylebone
1U53, 18:06 London Marylebone - Banbury

Interestingly, until the cessation of WSMR services in January 2011, the Chiltern Line was a hive of loco-hauled activity with Class 67s working **four** Chiltern Train services and **six** WSMR trains!

Diagram (1) : Formed of a Class 67 + WSMR Mk3s + DVT,
using two new bay platforms at Birmingham Moor Street station.

Diagram (2) : Class 67 + DVT No.82302 + Mk3 coaches hired in from Cargo D.

Another Outing, or Two!

In June 2011 (24th) and June 2013 (13th), I made two further trips (starting off, as usual, at Banbury) with the intention of visiting both London Marylebone and Birmingham Moor Street. On the 24th outing I also made one complete run between London and Birmingham behind No.67015, racking up 112 miles in the process.

As these loco-hauled services continued to operate, later with the excellent Class 68s, whenever I had to visit Birmingham or beyond, I would always endeavour to travel via Banbury and Birmingham, so I could enjoy some diesel haulage.

BANBURY (above) : *Class 67 No.67012 'A Shropshire Lad' is leading Chiltern Railways service 1H53, the 10:55 Birmingham Moor Street - London Marylebone, seen on the approach to Banbury. Usually, the Class 67 loco is at the northern end of the formation*

BANBURY (above) : *This time, No.67012 'A Shropshire Lad' is at the right end of the formation, as you can see in this view taken at the Banbury stop, while hauling 1R48, the 16:47 London Marylebone - Birmingham Moor Street. Note, the Chiltern-allocated Class 67s do not have their number displayed on the front end.*

BIRMINGHAM MOOR STREET (below) : *Take a trip down memory lane at Moor Street with plenty of railwayana on display: lamps, water crane and station canopy, complete with valence, painted in GWR chocolate / dark brown colour. Here, No.67015 'David J Lloyd' sits atop the stock in one of the restored bay platforms, ready to depart with 1H53, the 15:55hrs service to London Marylebone.*

A Slice of History

London Marylebone

The station opened to coal traffic in July 1898 and to passengers in March 1899, becoming the terminus of the Great Central Railway and the last major railway line to be built into London until High Speed 1. The station served High Wycombe, Aylesbury, Rugby, Leicester, Nottingham, Sheffield and Manchester and was the last, and smallest, of London's main line termini to be built, opening with half of the platforms originally planned.

From the mid-20th Century, traffic declined at Marylebone, especially after the GCR closed. By the 1980s, the station became rather run down, grubby, and was threatened with closure; it was only reprieved because of commuter traffic on the London to Aylesbury Line and from High Wycombe. In 1993, the station forged a new role as terminus of the Chiltern Main Line.

After the privatisation of British Rail in 1996, Chiltern Railways took over and improvements followed:

- introduction of loco-hauled trains using Mk3 stock. (From 2008)
- services extended to Birmingham Snow Hill and Kidderminster.
- 2015, services commenced between Marylebone and Oxford Parkway via a new chord at Bicester, serving Oxford as well a year later.

In connection with this, the main line was restored to double track and Marylebone station expanded in 2006 with two extra platforms as part of Chiltern railways 'Evergreen 2 project'. A shortened Platform 4 opened the same year along with two new platforms (5 and 6), built on the site of the old goods sidings on the west side of the station. A new depot was opened near Wembley Stadium.

LONDON MARYLEBONE

(above) : *Class 67 No.67012 'A Shropshire Lad' waits to leave the former Great Central Railway London terminus with 1R48, the 16:47 London Marylebone - Birmingham Moor Street, having earlier arrived with 1H53 from Birmingham Moor Street.*

The renovated trainshed, glass canopies and ironwork, are clear for all to see - a first class job indeed.

Birmingham Moor Street

Moor Street station opened in 1909 by the Great Western Railway as a terminus for local trains, followed by a newer Moor Street station with through platforms, opening in 1987.

At the beginning of the 21st Century, the Great Western Railway greatly expanded their facilities in Birmingham to cope with demand. Snow Hill station was extensively rebuilt and expanded, but the twin tracked Snow Hill tunnel did not have enough capacity to accommodate all of the traffic from the south. To solve the problem, Moor Street station was built at the opposite end of the tunnel to take terminating local trains from Leamington Spa, Stratford-upon-Avon via the recently opened North Warwickshire Line.

As an aside, electrification of the main line from London Euston to Birmingham New Street in the 1960s saw New Street favoured over Snow Hill and most of its services were withdrawn.

On 4th March 1968, the line between the junction with the Moor Street branch and Birmingham Snow Hill, including Snow Hill tunnel, closed. Snow Hill station finally closed in 1972, demolition followed five years later.

In the mid-1980s, funding enabled a new station to open at Birmingham Snow Hill, along with Snow Hill tunnel. As part of the reopening scheme, a new Moor Street station with through platforms was built at the southern portal of the restored tunnel. On completion of this project, the original Moor Street terminus became redundant, and closed down; the old platforms were disconnected from the network and a new through station came into use in October 1987.

Restoration : Interestingly, the original station was not demolished but mothballed and allowed to deteriorate, the former platforms becoming overgrown and dilapidated, not to mention visible cracks in the walls of the station buildings.

In March 1988, the ‘Moor Street Station Historical Society’ was formed to "Save Our Station".

Large teams of volunteers met each weekend to clean and preserve the various buildings, artifacts carefully renovated and stored for subsequent re-use for when the station reopened. As a result of their efforts, the old station became Grade II listed in 1998.

History would once again rise to the surface .... services on the Snow Hill lines became strained again, due to capacity issues through Snow Hill tunnel. This time, Chiltern Railways and the Birmingham Alliance decided to restore the original terminus at Moor Street and reopen it, allowing some services to terminate there rather than Snow Hill. Between 2002 and 2003 the original Moor Street station building and platforms were renovated and restored at a cost of £11 million.

The ‘new’ station, refurbished in 1930s style, has reproduction lamps, clock, seating, signage and GWR-style platform canopies.

However, there was a long delay before the old terminal platforms were connected to the network and opened for service, due to necessary signalling work to be carried out. Two of the three former terminal platforms (3 and 4) reopened for business on 11th December 2010 and the original station and the 1980s station, once again, combined into one.

67s Vice DMUs

A familiar story .... TOCs not having sufficient units to fulfill their timetable.

In 2010, First Great Western introduce two sets of loco and coaches - vice DMUs - instead of cancelling the services altogether, which was an extremely unpalatable and unacceptable proposition. The two sets would use Class 57/3s operating in top 'n' tail mode with Mk2 carriages between Cardiff and Paignton / Taunton but, due to the poor availability of one of the 57/3s, a Class 66 loco was hired-in from GBRf initially, before D B Schenker took control.

These trains became a magnet for haulage enthusiasts and, as the services settled down, top 'n' tail Class 67s became the normal *modus operandi*. The Two diagrams were:

Cardiff - Taunton

2D04,	07:28	Taunton - Bristol Parkway
2Y10,	09:13	Bristol Parkway - Weston super Mare
5U14,	10:09	Weston super Mare - Taunton
2U14,	11:02	Taunton - Cardiff Central
2C79,	14:00	Cardiff Central - Taunton
2U24,	16:16	Taunton - Cardiff Central
2C89,	19:00	Cardiff Central - Taunton

Cardiff - Paignton

2U02,	06:19	Bristol T. M. - Cardiff Central
2C67,	08:00	Cardiff Central - Paignton
2U20,	12:47	Paignton - Cardiff Central
2C85,	17:00	Cardiff Central - Taunton
2M68,	19:18	Taunton - Bristol T. M.

Seeing What's On Offer ....

At the time, I was still very busy with the publication of *'Freightmaster'* and compiling *'Loco Review'* and I did not spend as much time travelling on these services as I would have liked. I made do with three days in September 2010 to sample both diagrams, starting from either Bristol Temple Meads or Taunton, depending which diagram I was covering.

I purchased a South West rover ticket and this enabled me to travel on any four days in a given seven day period, although travel was not permitted before 09:00hrs. However, there was dispensation, in that I could leave Swindon at 08:30hrs on a London Paddington - Penzance service for the South West. Without this, I could not have met 2Y10 and 2C67 on the second leg of the diagrams.

On the Friday, I only made one run, and that was with No.67026 on the 2C67 service as far as Exeter St. Davids, as I wanted to travel on the branch lines to Barnstable and Exmouth for the first time.

These trains were an ideal day out and I only wished there were more like them.

PAIGNTON

(above) : *Wednesday, 15th September 2010, was a bright and sunny day, ideal for taking a trip to the seaside, Paignton on the Torbay Riviera was my chosen destination. After arriving behind No.67026, there was plenty of time to walk down Torbay Road to the esplanade for a spot of lunch (fish & chips, of course!) and be back at the station for my train to Cardiff at 13 minutes to one o'clock. Whilst on the seafront, I could see two oil tankers at anchor in the Bay awaiting their sailing instructions.*

Back at the station, the stock for train service 2U20 sits at Platform 2, No.67028 the lead loco now for the run to Cardiff Central, 147 miles and 60 chains away.

(opposite) : *Earlier, No.67028 is seen bringing the ECS into the station for the 12:47hrs service to Cardiff Central after being stabled in Goodrington Sands carriage sidings.*

On the far left, is the track of the Dartmouth Steam Railway, formerly known as the Paignton and Dartmouth Steam Railway, a 6 mile and 60 chains heritage railway on the former Great Western Railway branch line between Paignton and Kingswear. Many thousands of tourists and rail enthusiasts flock to the railway every year.

The line was originally built by the Dartmouth and Torbay Railway, opening fully to Kingswear in August 1864. Sadly, the line did not survive 'Beeching' and was officially closed on 28th October 1972, but subsequently sold to the Dart Valley Light Railway on 30th December 1972 and the rest, as they say, is history.

	Tuesday, 14th September 2010	
67020	Bristol T. Meads - Weston s Mare	2Y10, 09:12 Bristol Parkway - Weston s Mare
67019	Bridgwater - Cardiff Central	2U14, 11:02 Taunton - Cardiff Central
67020	Cardiff Central - Taunton	2C79, 14:00 Cardiff Central - Taunton
67019	Taunton - Bristol T. Meads	2U24, 16:16 Taunton - Cardiff Central
	Wednesday, 15th September 2010	
67026	Taunton - Paignton	2C67, 08:00 Cardiff Central - Paignton
67028	Paignton - Cardiff Central	2U20, 12:47 Paignton - Cardiff Central
	Friday, 17th September 2010	
67026	Taunton - Exeter St Davids	2C67, 08:00 Cardiff Central - Paignton

Enter The "Cat"

Chiltern Railways sub-leased six DRS Class 68s, effective from December 2014, to replace Class 67s on Chiltern main line services between London Marylebone and Birmingham Moor Street / Snow Hill. Liveried in two-tone grey and silver bodyside with blue stripes, the 68s (nicknamed 'cats' by enthusiasts) certainly look the part.

They are fitted with Association of American Railroads (AAR) push-pull equipment to allow them to operate with Mk 3 coaching stock, along with two DRS-liveried locos (Nos.68008 and 68009) which act as stand-by in the event of any failures.

Sampling The Goods

I first paid a visit to the Chiltern Main Line on 11th June 2015, setting off from the now obligatory starting point at Banbury, but the day did not pan out as I planned. I made my way, this time, by train from Swindon with my wife who was travelling on to Birmingham International to attend the Gardeners' World Live Exhibition at the NEC; I was going to join her later in the day.

It all went well to start with, No.68012 pulled into Platform 2 with 1R22, the 10:15 London Marylebone - Birmingham Moor Street and the 'cat' exploded into action and off we went. Although, only a 20-mile journey, I decided to get off at Leamington Spa and await the next service north - 1G25, the 10:45 London Marylebone - Birmingham Snow Hill.

After a 30 minute wait, I boarded this service and decided to stay with No.68013 for the run to Snow Hill, return with it back to Leamington, where I would alight and make my way to Birmingham International using a Cross Country Voyager and meet my wife.

However, I soon realised that all was not well, the loco did not seem able to maintain any power, but I had no reason to think that this was only temporary and that it would reach Birmingham. Unfortunately, the train limped into Warwick station - an unscheduled stop - and there it stayed for about 20/25 minutes, in the hope the driver could find the fault and rectify it.

Sadly, it was not to be and passengers were told to detrain, there was an air leak somewhere in the set. The train eventually departed as ECS to Moor Street and passengers had no alternative but to await the next DMU north to continue their journey. Such an inauspicious start!

Since then, I have had some great runs with these excellent locos and I have included a small selection of images for your interest.

LONDON MARYLEBONE

(above) : *No.68014 sits at London Marylebone station having arrived with 1H55, the 13:12hrs service from Birmingham Snow Hill. This proved to be the only time I completed a full journey between the two cities.*

BANBURY

(opposite) : *After visiting the Severn Valley Railway to attend their 2015 'Steam Gala', I made way home from Kidderminster via the 'Jewellery Line' to Birmingham Moor Street and catch a Class 68 hauled service as far as Banbury. At Banbury, I photographed No.68010 departing with 1H69, the 15:55 Birmingham Moor St - London Marylebone. The semaphores went in 2016 when Banbury was resignalled to Multiple Aspect Signalling (MAS).*

The 68s

I really like these locos - they look good, sound good and are powerfully good too!

The Class 68 is a mainline mixed traffic diesel-electric loco manufactured by Stadler Rail (and previously by Vossloh España) for DRS, a design derived from the Stadler Eurolight, this variant being the UKLight. On the freight side, they work mainly Flask trains and intermodals, but many have been sub-contracted out by DRS to Train Operating Companies for passenger services

The first Class 68 to arrive in the UK was, in fact, No.68002 'Intrepid' in January 2014; No.68001 'Evolution' spent much of 2014 being tested at the Velim test centre in the Czech Republic. Between 2013 - 2017 a total of 34 locos were built, most of which carried names, broadly following a naval theme.

The 68s are allocated, thus:

Direct Rail Services	:	68001 - 68005	68008, 68009	68016 - 68018	68033, 68034
ScotRail	:	68006, 68007			
Chiltern Railways	:	68010 - 68015			
Trans Pennine Express	:	68010 - 68032.			

LEAMINGTON SPA

This delightful station is located on the site of the first through-station in Leamington, opened by the Great Western Railway on its new line from Birmingham to Oxford in 1852.

The London and North Western Railway had reached Leamington eight years earlier, in 1844, with a branch from Coventry, but that line terminated about 1.5 miles from the town centre, at Milverton.

The station was refurbished in early 2008 to resemble the original Great Western Railway art-deco style, including GWR-style posters, lamps and running in boards *(see left)* at the south end of platforms 2 and 3, plus beautifully maintained flower beds.

Leamington Spa is a popular spot these days for enthusiasts with a wealth of freight and Class 68 loco-hauled passenger activity.

(top) : No.68015 is seen arriving at Leamington Spa with 1R25, the 11;10 London Marylebone - Birmingham Moor Street.

(middle / left) : *Leamington railwayana.*

(above) : *For my trip on 21st October 2015, I was greeted at Banbury by the arrival of 1R22, the 10:15 London Marylebone - Birmingham Moor Street, hauled by DRS liveried Class 68 No.68008 'Avenger', a pleasant change from the usual diet of Chiltern Railways liveried locos. Here, No.68008 'Avenger' stands at Leamington, where I alighted to wait for No.68014 and a run to Snow Hill.*

(below) : *"Two for the price of one" .... three years later and 68s cross paths at Leamington Spa. No.68013 awaits departure time with 1R21, the 10:10 London Marylebone - Birmingham Moor Street, just as No.68014 arrives, propelling 1H33, the 10:55 Birmingham Moor Street - London Marylebone into Platform 2.*

SOLIHULL (above) : *On 20th March 2018, I spent the day doing the 68s with my old friend Michael, who had not previously done so. We had an enjoyable day and spent two trips with No.68013 and No.68015, the latter of which is seen waiting at Solihull with 1H45, the 12:55 Birmingham Moor Street - London Marylebone.*

BIRMINGHAM SNOW HILL (below) : *This is Snow Hill today, completely unrecognisable to GWR times, modern glass fronted buildings overlook the station and even the platform shelters have a modern, futuristic, look about them. I have arrived behind No.68014 on 1G25, the 10;45hrs service from Marylebone, which I will stay with for the run back to the Capital - the 13:12hrs service, reporting code 1H55.*

BIRMINGHAM MOOR STREET

(above) : *68010 sits in Platform 3 bay platform, having arrived with 1R33, the 13:10hrs service from London Marylebone. Note, Platform 5 is not in use, only bays 3 and 4 are.*

(below) : *This was that fateful day in June 2015, when No.68013 and its train (1G25) gave up the ghost at Warwick, where passengers were forced to leave the train. Having proceeded as ECS to Birmingham, the ensemble is seen receiving attention by a fitter. At the same time, Class 165 2-car Network Turbo DMU No.165 009 arrives with 2R28, the 12:32 Leamington Spa - Birmingham Moor Street.*

"My Favourite Journey"

Setting The Scene

The year was 1980, the date 5th April, and I fondly recall enjoying a ride behind my favourite Class of loco, a Class 40. It manifested itself in the shape of No.40116, which worked a charter from Carnforth to Maryport and return.

Maryport was the northern limit of travel for the train because of restricted clearances on the section of line between Maryport and Carlisle; several overbridges were built to narrower dimensions by the Maryport & Carlisle Railway, which opened the line in 1845.

(above) : *No.40116 at Maryport.*

At the time, Class 108 first generation DMUs working this route were custom-fitted with bars on the drop-light doors, thus preventing passengers from "sticking their head out of the window and losing it" - a little melodramatic maybe, but that was the reality!

In future years, Class 150 and Class 158 DMUs, for example, have also been banned from the route, but Class 142, 153 and Class 156 units are allowed.

I always planned to revisit the line one day, especially to complete the 'missing link' from Maryport to Carlisle, but DMU-only travel on this route was not an attractive proposition and, furthermore, it was a very long way from Swindon.

However, that was all going to change ......

Cometh the May 2015 Timetable Change

Between May 2015 and 28th December 2018, a number of scheduled services were introduced between Carlisle & Barrow in Furness, using Mk2 coaches and Class 37 diesel locos hired in from Direct Rail Services, working in top 'n' tail formation. The aim was to provide additional seating capacity and the coaches had all been modified to include bars across the droplight windows.

This new schedule appealed to me greatly and was something I would definitely sample, as and when publishing commitments allowed. It actually turned out that the first of several such trips took place in July 2016; more of this later.

A Little History

The Cumbrian Coast line in North West England, runs from Carlisle to Barrow-in-Furness via Workington and Whitehaven, which continues (as the Furness line) via Ulverston and Grange-over-Sands to Carnforth, where it connects with the West Coast Main Line.

George Stephenson initially envisaged linking England and Scotland by a railway running along the coast between Lancaster and Carlisle, but this 'Grand Caledonian Junction Railway' was never built, the direct route over Shap being preferred. To give you an idea of the present day difference:

Route		Miles	No. of Stations	Travel Time
Lancaster to Carlisle	WCML	69	2	1 Hr.
Lancaster to Carlisle	Cumbrian Coast	141	32	3 Hrs. 30 mins.

Consequently, the Cumbrian coast line is an amalgamation of four different railway companies:

Maryport and Carlisle Railway

Intended to link with the Newcastle and Carlisle Railway to give a continuous line linking the Irish Sea and the North Sea, it opened fully between Maryport and Carlisle in 1845.

Whitehaven Junction Railway

The first station at Whitehaven was opened in March 1847 as the terminus of their line from Maryport, to the south of the present station. The line from Maryport to Workington actually opened in November 1845, Harrington May 1846 with full opening to passengers in March 1847. Between Whitehaven and Harrington the line runs between the cliffs and the sea, to this day rockfalls, landslips and high tides make this a vulnerable section of the route.

Whitehaven and Furness Junction Railway

On the southern side of Whitehaven, the first section of the Whitehaven and Furness Junction Railway (W&FJR) opened in June 1849 from a terminus at Whitehaven (Preston Street) to Ravenglass, but there was no connection between this line and the Whitehaven Junction Railway. To remedy this, a tunnel 1,333 yards long was built, completed in 1852. In 1854, W&FJR passenger trains began using the WJR station at Whitehaven. The line was extended to Bootle in 1850 and to Foxfield in November the same year.

Furness Railway

In the early 1840s, the owners of iron ore mines in the Furness district wanted a 'waggonway', promoted by the Dukes of Buccleuch and Devonshire, to carry iron (at Dalton-in-Furness) and slate (at Kirkby-in-Furness) to Barrow harbour; its docks opening in 1867. For the record, by 1867 there were eleven blast furnaces in operation at Barrow, boasting the largest Bessemer steel works in the country and one of the largest in the world.

In 1848, the Furness Railway extended its line from Barrow-in-Furness to Kirkby-in-Furness. Two years later, the Whitehaven & Furness Junction Railway completed its line from Whitehaven to join the Furness Railway from Barrow at Foxfield, making it a junction of some importance.

Two years later, the Whitehaven & Furness Junction Railway completed its line down the coast from Whitehaven to join the FR line from Barrow, making Foxfield a junction by Broughton-in-Furness, principally to serve local copper mines. Two years later, the Whitehaven & Furness Junction Railway completed its line down the coast from Whitehaven, joining the line from Barrow.

The original main line did not run through Barrow, through trains had to run into a terminal station and then out again. A new Barrow Central railway station opened in 1882, when through working became possible after the opening of a new loop line, over which the Whitehaven- Carnforth passenger traffic now runs.

All the above constituents were absorbed into the London, Midland and Scottish Railway in 1923.

The Furness Line

This narrative would not be complete without reference to the Furness Line, which runs from Barrow-in-Furness to Lancaster, joining the WCML at Carnforth. The line opened in stages between 1846 and 1857.

Along with the Cumbrian Coast Line, the route is considered one of the most scenic in England, especially between Silverdale and Ulverston where the line, for the most part, skirts Morecambe Bay.

The mountains of the Lake District are never far from view through the carriage window and the line crosses the impressive Kent and Leven viaducts along the way. This line became an important artery for me, linking the southern end of the Cumbrian Coast Line with Preston.

I must agree, this line is equally as impressive as the Cumbrian Main Line with it's stunning views.

The Start - 21st July 2016

The main reason for this trip was not just to travel the entirety of the Cumbrian Coast Line, but to be in Carlisle to see 4-6-2 Pacific No.46229 'Duchess of Sutherland' work in on a 'Cumbrian Mountain Express'. This was specially so for my friend Graham, who travelled with me.

For a change, we decided to arrive in Carlisle by way of a somewhat roundabout route:

1st Leg :	17:16hrs -	Aviva Class 67 from Cardiff Central to Chester - overnight stay.	(1W96)
2nd Leg :	08:52hrs -	Class 175 DMU from Chester to Warrington Bank Quay.	(1H83)
3rd Leg :	09:28hrs -	Pendolino to Preston.	(9S44)
4th Leg :	10:04hrs -	Class 37/4 to Barrow-in-Furness.	(2C47)
5th Leg :	11:40hrs -	Class 37/4 To Carlisle.	(2C49)

All's Well ?

Well, yes and no.

The day started off well, as Class 67 No.67002 (required for haulage!) pulled into Platform 2 at Cardiff Central with the 17:16hrs service to Holyhead. The train was routed via the 'Marches' from Newport to Shrewsbury, then via Wrexham to Chester, where the train is scheduled to reverse for the remaining miles to Holyhead.

An overnight stay at a Premier Inn, 200 yards walk from the station was pre-arranged. Arrival at Chester was 2-minutes shy of eight o'clock, leaving plenty of time for an evening meal and a glass of wine - very civilised and a long way from my 'bashing' days of the early 80s when travelling through the night was the norm.

After a cooked breakfast, we made our way to the station for the train to Warrington Bank Quay - Class 175 No.175 110 arrived and departed bang on time destined for Manchester Airport. How I was so glad I did not have to commute to work everyday. The train was wedged, without a seat to spare, commuters standing in the passageway since joining the train at Chester along with those joining the train at 'pick up' points after leaving Llandudno.

(above) : *No.67002 arrives at Cardiff Central with the stock to form 1W96 to Holyhead.*

(above) : *Semaphores, gantry and Crewe Junction signal box at Shrewsbury station.*

Now things start to go wrong ....

After picking up passengers at Runcorn East, the next stop would be Warrington Bank Quay. However, as the train was about to pass over the WCML, near Daresbury, we came to a stop.

After what seemed an eternity, but probably only about five minutes in reality, the train manager announced over the tannoy that there had been a signal failure just south of Acton Grange Junction and we would have to wait for a path into Bank Quay station. As the wait lengthened, the train we were due to catch at Warrington (9S44) sped northwards on the WCML below.

We had missed our connection ....

There was no alternative but to recast our schedule, which would now be:

10:14hrs	:	Warrington Bank Quay - Preston	Pendolino	(1S45)
10:45hrs	:	Preston to Barrow-in-Furness	Class 185 No.185 142	(1C52)
14:37hrs	:	Barrow-in-Furness to Carlisle	Class 37/4 No.37402	(2C41)

So, this was the new plan and to say that I was annoyed, was an understatement, I was seriously 'Pxxxed Off'. It just had to happen today, didn't it and to rub salt into the wound, there would be a two and a half hour wait at Barrow before our train left for Carlisle. Happy days.....

Eventually, DBSO No.9704 led the stock and Class 37 No.**37402 'Stephen Middlemore'** out of Barrow Carriage Sidings and into Platform 2 in plenty of time for the 14:37hrs departure to Carlisle.

Shortly after leaving Barrow-in-Furness, the sky darkened and rain started to fall heavily, which persisted for most of the journey to Carlisle. I wanted to take some photographs en-route, but a combination of bad weather and barred droplight windows made this difficult.

BARROW-in-FURNESS

(above) : Class 37/4 No.37402 'Stephen Middlemore' prepares to leave for the carriage sidings, which is the loco and stock off 2C47, the train we should have caught had our plans not been scuppered at Warrington. At the far end of Platform 1, Class 185 No.185 142 is seen leaving with a service bound for Manchester Airport.

Reminiscences

I know they say "time flies', but it's only when you reflect that you realise how true a statement this really is.

With this in mind, I looked back over my records and found that I had not been to Barrow for more than 30 years, in fact, on two separate occasions.

(middle) : **5th April 1980**

During a railtour, which featured No.40116 working a Carnforth - Maryport - Carnforth leg of a railtour, a 'photostop' was arranged at Barrow for the passengers.

For some unknown reason, I did not photograph No.40116 (perhaps, too many people in the way!) but sought out the old bay platform, where two locos were stabled; Class 40 No.40112 and an unidentified Class 25.

(left) : **9th August 1984**

This was the only time I travelled on a British Rail timetabled service train to Barrow, loco-hauled, and with a Class 40 loco, no less!

Here, 1P11, the 11:15hrs service from Liverpool Lime Street has arrived with No.40013 'Andania' in charge, which will 'run round' and leave with 1K32, the 15:24hrs service to Crewe, with me onboard.

Semaphores and Signal Box

(above) : *A British Rail (London Midland Region) bracket signal sits at the northern end of Platform 2 and Platform 1, respectively, at Barrow-in-Furness station.*

This is a standard structure, mounted on a tall main post with a welded girder structure forming the platform. The main signal ('doll') is at a higher level and is for access to the main line, while the smaller 'doll' gives access to the sidings. Note the weight bars, which are accessed from the same ladder.

(below) : *DBSO No.9704 leads the coaches and loco from the carriage sidings into the station, which will form 2C41, the 14:37 Barrow in Furness - Carlisle.*

"Through the Carriage Window"

Barrow Docks (above) : *On the approach to Barrow-in-Furness, I looked out across Cavendish Dock reservoir to Ramsden Dock, where all three of the PNTL (Pacific Nuclear Transport Limited) fleet were berthed: 'Pacific Egret', 'Pacific Heron' and 'Pacific Grebe'. These three vessels ship used nuclear fuel, vitrified high-level waste, mixed oxide (MOX) fuel and plutonium around the world.*

Seascale (below) : *This image gives you an idea of how murky the weather conditions were on the way to Carlisle, although this did not deter golfers playing a round of golf at Seascale Golf Club. In the background, the skyline is dominated with chimneys and other structures at the Sellafield Nuclear Reprocessing Plant.*

Tanyard Bay, Parton (above) : *Cormorants sit on the rocks, hoping for some sunshine to dry their wings - no chance, today! The shoreline is rocky between Parton and Workington, the railway line twists and turns hugging the cliffs along the way.*

Workington (middle) : *As my train pulled away from Workington, I grabbed this 'record' shot of Workington Main No.3 signal box at the north end of the 'Up' platform. It's representative of the London and North Western Railway type 4 'box, which opened in 1886 equipped with a 55 lever bar and stud locked LNWR tumbler frame.*

Sellafield (below) : *I noticed several DRS locos stabled for their next nuclear flask trains, including Class 66 No.66301 and Class 57 No.57003, along with a water crane from a bygone era.*

"Portrait of a Duchess"

LMS Coronation Class 4-6-2 Pacific - No.46233 'Duchess of Sutherland'

(above) : *This is what we came to Carlisle to see, No.46233 'Duchess of Sutherland' arrive with 'The Cumbrian Mountain Express', running as 1Z62, the 08:20 Crewe - Carlisle. The charter had earlier set off from Crewe (1Z61) working to Liverpool Lime Street behind Class 37 No.37706, where another 37, No.37668, worked back to Crewe.*

They say a picture is better than a 1,000 words so, in which case, the next few images need no explanation.

CUMBRIAN
MOUNTAIN
EXPRESS
46233

DUCHESS OF SUTHERLAND

CUMBRIAN
MOUNTAIN
EXPRESS
46233

CUMBRIAN MOUNTAIN EXPRESS
46233
CE 296
CE 297

COLAS RAIL FREIGHT
20

(above) : *The doyen member of the DRS Class 37/4 fleet, No.37401 'Mary Queen of Scots' is seen arriving at Carlisle with 2C47, the 17:31hrs service from Barrow-in-Furness. Colas Class 37 No.37219 is stabled in High Wapping Sidings, having worked a Network Rail test train from Derby.*

(Previous Page) : *Colas replaced DB Schenker as traction provider for petroleum trains running out of Grangemouth refinery to terminals at Linkswood, Prestwick (both in Scotland) and Dalston. At 06:50hrs on Saturday, 23rd July 2016, Colas 'tug' No.60095 passes Carlisle North Junction with 6C35, the 07:37 Carlisle Yard - Dalston loaded tanks; a portion off the main train, 6M34, the 21:29 (Fri) Grangemouth - Dalston.*

(below) : *Standing at the north end of Platform 8 at Carlisle Citadel station, I 'photted' 'Powerhaul' Class 70 No.70002 about to pass through with 4M27, the 0:525 Coatbridge - Daventry freightliner.*

CARLISLE

"One of my all time favourite locations"

(above) : *It's Saturday morning and still pretty murky overhead, but there is sufficient light to record a pair of DRS Class 68s, No.68018 + No.68004 working 4S43, the 06:40 Daventry - Mossend 'Tesco Express' intermodal.*

(below) : *Seen previously stabled at Sellafield, Class 66 No.66305 + Class 57 No.57003 now double-head a single flask, which is running as 6C46, the 12:56 Sellafield - Carlisle Kingmoor.*

The Windermere Branch

The Windermere branch is 10 miles and 15 chains of single track, opening in April 1847, originally built as the Kendal and Windermere Railway, connecting into the Lancaster and Carlisle Railway at Oxenholme. At the 1923 Grouping, it became part of the London, Midland and Scottish Railway.

(above) : *My train (2C16, the 15:34 Oxenholme - Windermere) stands at Platform 3 ready to leave, formed of Class 156 No.156 468 (leading) and Class 153 No.153 360 at the rear.*

(below) : *At Windermere, No.156 468 stands with its rear lights showing 'red' as No.153 360 will lead the 16:00hrs service (2C17) back to Oxenholme, with very few passengers, it would seem, boarding.*

"A Poor Decision"

On 5th July 2017, I decided to combine the 37s on the Cumbrian Coast followed by an afternoon's jaunt along the WCML to Oxenholme, in order to travel along the Windermere branch for the first time, returning to Preston via Carlisle and Barrow-in-Furness.

To cut a long story short, the day went extremely well, just as I had planned, except that I had not studied the timetable, presuming there would be a connecting service straightaway from Barrow-in-Furness back to Preston, after the arrival of my train (2C42) from Carlisle - a lesson I should have learnt from August 1975, when I got stranded at Inverness without a train south!

After visiting Windermere, I arrived back in Carlisle courtesy of a Class 350 EMU working from Manchester Airport to Edinburgh Waverley.

I had about 20-minutes to wait before my train to Barrow and took this shot of Colas Class 67 No.67023 *(inset)* working a STP 1Q18, Heaton - York test train with No.67026 on the rear.

You can see the scaffolding in place ready for the trainshed roof and glass panels to be replaced.

At this stage, it's worth appreciating the logistics of completing a journey from Carlisle to Barrow. As rewarding as this route may be in terms of breathtaking views though the carriage window, along with the mesmerizing throb of a Class 37, it can get a little tiring, especially if you decide to do the Barrow - Carlisle - Barrow 'out & back' trip in one go. For this reason, many loco-bashers do small sections at a time, interchanging between the two loco diagrams.

A few facts might put this in perspective:

Route Miles	: 85 miles 60 chains
Stations	: 24
Journey Time	: 2 hours 45 minutes

"*Ghost Train*"

After leaving Ravenglass, I decided to see how many passengers were still on the train and, to my complete surprise, the train was empty *(see inset),* I was literally last man standing.

When I arrived at Barrow (20:29hrs), I was horrified to see there was no connection onwards to Preston for nearly two hours. Unbelievably, the previous train to Preston departed five minutes before my arrival. Why, oh why, was this service not held for 2C42's arrival?

Perhaps, as no passengers alighted, save for myself, this was the reason for no connection. In which case, why didn't 2C42 run as far as Whitehaven, and ECS thereafter?

I must say that Barrow-in-Furness railway station was eerily empty and unappealing at this time of night and I felt somewhat vulnerable. The unit to Preston was equally empty and, had it been cancelled, which is not entirely out of the question where Northern Rail is concerned, I would have been stranded in Barrow.

Summary of Journeys

Friday, 22nd July 2016

37402	Barrow in Furness - Carlisle	2C41, 14:37	Barrow in Furness - Carlisle

Saturday, 23rd July 2016

37402	Carlisle - Whitehaven	2C40, 08:42	Carlisle - Barrow in Furness
37401	Whitehaven - Carlisle	2C41, 08:45	Barrow in Furness - Carlisle

Wednesday, 5th July 2017

37403	Preston - Barrow in Furness	2C47, 10:04	Preston - Barrow in Furness
37425	Barrow in Furness - Carlisle	2C49, 11:40	Barrow in Furness - Carlisle
37403	Carlisle - Barrow in Furness	2C42, 17:37	Carlisle - Barrow in Furness

Saturday, 23rd September 2017

37422	Lancaster - Carnforth	2C31, 17:31	Lancaster - Barrow in Furness

Monday, 25th September 2017

37402	Preston - Barrow in Furness	2C47, 10:04	Preston - Barrow in Furness
37422	Barrow in Furness - Carlisle	2C49, 11:40	Barrow in Furness - Carlisle
37422	Carlisle - Whitehaven	2C34, 14:35	Carlisle - Barrow in Furness
37402	Whitehaven - Carlisle	2C41, 14:37	Barrow in Furness - Carlisle

Monday, 7th May 2018

68003	Preston - Barrow in Furness	2C47, 10:04	Preston - Barrow in Furness
37402	Barrow in Furness - Carlisle	2C49, 11:40	Barrow in Furness - Carlisle
37402	Carlisle - Whitehaven	2C34, 14:35	Carlisle - Barrow in Furness
68004	Whitehaven - Carlisle	2C41, 14:37	Barrow in Furness - Carlisle

Tuesday, 8th May 2018

37402	Preston - Barrow in Furness	2C47, 10:04	Preston - Barrow in Furness
68003	Barrow in Furness - Carlisle	2C49, 11:40	Barrow in Furness - Carlisle
68004	Carlisle - Whitehaven	2C34, 14:35	Carlisle - Barrow in Furness
37402	Whitehaven - Carlisle	2C41, 14:37	Barrow in Furness - Carlisle

---

Notes : Each Class 37-hauled set ran with a DBSO (Driving Brake Standard Open).
The driver in the DBSO can drive the loco, even though it is at the rear of the train.

The Class 68s run in top 'n' tail formation

Cumbrian Coast Loco-Hauled Diagrams

Diagram 1

5C32,	04;56	Carlisle Kingmoor DRS - Carlisle	ECS
2C32,	05:15	Carlisle - Preston	
2C47,	10:04	Preston - Barrow in Furness	
5C47,	11:42	Barrow in Furness - Barrow CS	
5C41,	14:25	Barrow CS - Barrow in Furness	ECS
2C41,	14:37	Barrow in Furness - Carlisle	
2C42,	17:37	Carlisle - Barrow in Furness	
5C42,	20:38	Barrow in Furness - Barrow CS	ECS

Diagram 2

5C33,	05:34	Barrow CS - Barrow in Furness	ECS
2C33,	05:46	Barrow in Furness - Carlisle	
2C40,	08:42	Carlisle - Barrow in Furness	
2C49,	11;40,	Barrow in Furness - Carlisle	
2C34,	14;35	Carlisle - Barrow in Furness	
2C47,	17:31	Barrow in Furness - Carlisle	
5C47,	20:41	Carlisle - Carlisle Kingmoor DRS	ECS

Notes : The diagrams interchange after each weekday, so:
The loco and set off Diagram 1 (5C42) forms Diagram 2 the next day (5C33)
The loco and set off Diagram 2 (5C47) forms Diagram 1 the next day (5C32)

Cumbrian Coast Anecdote

This railway line is simply stunning, as is the section of Furness Line between Carnforth and Ulverston.

I like the whole route, especially the section between Whitehaven to Harrington, where the railway line hugs the contours of the cliffs perched precariously on the shoreline of the Solway Firth. In fact, during my research, I came across an article which I feel sums up this railway to good effect.

When the Whitehaven – Harrington section opened, the *'Carlisle Journal'* reported:

"Zig-zag, zig-zag, zig-zag, perpetually. No serpent wriggles in more contortions than the Whitehaven Junction Railway" .... pointing out the horrors of an accident on such a corniche.

"The poor wretches who fill the train must either have their brains dashed out against the rocks at one side or be pitched head-foremost into the sea on the other"

Train crew could never see far ahead, and there was always the possibility of a rockfall onto the track: even after the doubling of the line, the Board of Trade required a speed limit of 15 mph on the section.

(Overleaf)

(page 204) : ***No.37403*** *'Isle of Mull' pulls into Platform 1 at Carlisle Citadel station with 2C41, the 14:37 Barrow in Furness - Carlisle, which will form my train service back to Barrow at 17:37hrs.*

(page 205) : ***No.37403*** *is seen again, this time in beautiful, early evening, light upon arrival at Barrow with 2C42, the 17:37hrs service from Carlisle.*

1
10 9/11
37403
CE313
996

Enter the '68s' ....

April 2018

The Class 37s working the two Cumbrian Coast diagrams are now 60 years old and they are showing their age in terms of reliability. Since being introduced on the route, there have been many failures, resulting in loco-replacement, DMU substitutes, or even service cancellations.

To remedy the situation, DRS replace one of the Class 37/4 diagrams with two Class 68s, running in top 'n' tail formation. Two 'cats' are needed, as a single Class 68 cannot work with a DBSO, although one will be retained in the train set.

The two diagrams will interchange as before, so the locos working Diagram 1 on one day will then work Diagram 2 the next day.

7th / 8th May 2018

I knew these loco-hauled services on the Cumbrian Coast would not go on forever, maybe until the end of 2018 at the latest. With electrification projects proceeding well in Scotland, redundant DMUs would be cascaded to displace the loco-hauled sets. There was no time like the present, so I decided to go and enjoy these services before it was to late.

I stayed at a Premier Inn in Preston, my usual haunt, within a 10-minute walk of the railway station, convenient as my starting point each morning would be:

2C47, the 10:04 Preston - Barrow in Furness

With the interchanging of diagrams, each day started with:

7th May : **68003**

8th May : **37402**

Train 2C47 was an excellent service, connecting at Barrow-in-Furness for another loco-hauled service to Carlisle (2C49), which would be No.37402 on the 7th and No.68003 on the 8th.

Furthermore, 2C47 was well patronised and the times I worked it, the front coach was always crowded with enthusiasts. The operating authorities knew this and, to their credit, would hold 2C49 if 2C47 was running a few minutes late - they were even known on occasions to cancel 2C49 and run 2C47 straight through to Carlisle, if latenesss necessitated.

2C47 was a good revenue-earner for the TOCs and it was to my astonishment this train was removed from the start of the Summer Timetable, resulting in the remaining loco-hauled services simply running between Barrow and Carlisle. This single action slashed interest in these trains at a stroke, as a DMU from Preston to Barrow was not an attractive proposition to start the day, nor was a venture to Carlisle.

So, as it turned out, my timing was fortuitous and was my last visit to the Cumbrian Coast.

I have included some images from these two days travel for your interest and I hope you enjoy reading about my exploits, as much as I have in writing about it.

(Opposite)

(top) : *On 7th May, No.68004 enters Platform 5 at Preston station with 2C32, the 05:15 Carlisle - Preston, which has come via Barrow-in-Furness, No.68003 tails the formation, out of view.*

This set will form 2C47, the 10:04 Preston - Barrow in Furness, led by No.68004.

A Virgin Pendolino waits at Platform 4 with 1S42, the 07:10 London Euston - Glasgow Central.

(bottom) : *On 8th May 2018, No.68004 sits at Carlisle and my train service (2C34) to Whitehaven.*

PN
131
PN
132
Virgin
68004
10
9/11

1
68004

"The Fill In Move"

(above) : *After arriving at Carlisle off the 11:40hrs service from Barrow-in-Furness, there was sufficient time to do another trip, this time to Whitehaven and back, although some 'bashers' went further south for a connection. The journey was about one hour and another 39 miles and 60 chains haulage, each way.*

No.68003 propels 2C34 the 14:35hrs ex-Carlisle) into Whitehaven Tunnel, departing from Platform 2, which is now bi-directional. Platform 1 (to the right and out of view) is now a bay platform, whilst the former platforms (3 and 4) are now completely disused and, as you can see, the track has been lifted.